Relationship harmony through mindfulness.

Josie J. Jackson

ALL RIGHTS RESERVED.

Abstract

Conflict is not only inevitable in a romantic relationship, but also a primary predictor of relationship satisfaction and commitment. The purpose of this quantitative correlational study was to examine if and to what extent a correlation exists between the five mechanisms of mindfulness identified in the Five Facet Mindfulness Questionnaire and the conflict strategy subdomains identified in the Romantic Partner Conflict Scale as used by adults in a committed romantic relationship living in the mid-Atlantic region of the US. Jon Kabat-Zinn's model of mindfulness and Albert Chavannes's social exchange theory serve as the theoretical foundations for this study. An anonymous sample of adults in a committed romantic relationship living in the mid-Atlantic region of the US ($N = 103$) completed a self-report survey. The survey consisted of seven demographic questions (two required, five optional), 15 items from the FFMQ-15, and 39 items from the RPCS. Following assumptions testing and descriptive analysis, the observing facet of mindfulness was omitted due to low reliability using Cronbach's alpha. The remaining four facets of mindfulness and six conflict strategy subdomains were analyzed using Kendall's Tau-b. The correlation analysis yielded the following statistically significant correlations: acting with awareness/interactional reactivity ($\tau_b(103) = -.230$, $p = .002$), acting with awareness/domination ($\tau_b(103) = -.195$, $p = .007$), describing/compromise ($\tau_b(103) = .241$, $p < .001$), describing/interactional reactivity ($\tau_b(103) = -.209$, $p = .004$), describing/domination ($\tau_b(103) = -.264$, $p < .001$), non-judging/interactional reactivity ($\tau_b(103) = -.274$, $p < .001$), and non-judging/domination ($\tau_b(103) = -.350$, $p < .001$). These findings serve as the basis for novel research and practical recommendations.

Keywords: mindfulness, adult, romantic, conflict, partners, relationships

Dedication

It is with unending gratitude that I dedicate this dissertation to all the teachers in my life. You help me see my strengths and push me to be better. My first lesson in balance. Thank you.

Acknowledgments

With an overflowing heart (and eyes), I recognize the immeasurable contribution of so many who supported my journey. First, my husband, Kyle, who encouraged me to start my doctoral journey some 3 years ago and has walked side by side with me every step since then. My mother, who taught me not what to think, but how to think critically and where to find the answers. Erika Melton, my middle school science teacher, who instilled in me a love of learning and insatiable curiosity. Next, my outstanding committee without whom I could never have completed this dissertation. Thank you, Dr. Hiebel, for your support, presence, guidance, and reality checks. Lord knows I need them. Thank you, Dr. Street, for your patience, clear explanations, and diligence. Thank you, Dr. Hill, for your kindness, excitement, and mentorship. Dr. Casteel, my quality reviewer, whose keen eye, and high standards make me proud to have made it this far. I would be remiss if I didn't also acknowledge Dr. Markette, Dr. Taffer, and Dr. Quade whose guidance at residency was inspirational and just absolutely spot on. I consider myself blessed to be surrounded by role models of such grace and wisdom.

Table of Contents

List of Tables xiii

List of Figures xiv

Chapter 1: Introduction to the Study 1

    Introduction 1

    Background of the Study 2

    Definition of Terms 4

    Anticipated Limitations 6

    Summary and Organization of the Remainder of the Study 7

Chapter 2: Literature Review 10

    Introduction to the Chapter and Background to the Problem 10

        Background 11

    Identification of the Problem Space 13

    Theoretical Foundations 16

        Social Exchange Theory 16

        Kabat-Zinn's Model of Mindfulness 19

    Review of the Literature 21

        Couples in a Romantic Relationship 22

        Conflict Strategies 35

        Mindfulness 43

        Points of Convergence 54

    Problem Statement 60

    Summary 62

Chapter 3: Methodology 64

Introduction 64

Purpose of the Study 65

Research Questions and Hypotheses 66

    Variables 72

Rationale for a Quantitative Methodology 77

Rationale for Research Design 78

Population and Sample Selection 80

    Quantitative Sample Size 81

    Recruiting and Sampling Strategy 82

Instrumentation 84

    Research Data 84

    Additional Data 89

Validity 91

Reliability 96

Data Collection and Management 98

Data Analysis Procedures 100

    Organizing and Cleaning 105

    Descriptive Statistical Analysis 106

    Scale Reliability 106

    Testing Assumptions 107

    Testing Research Hypotheses 109

Ethical Considerations 112

Assumptions and Delimitations 114

    Assumptions 114

Delimitations 115

Summary 116

Chapter 4: Data Analysis and Results 119

Introduction 119

Important Changes and Updates to Information in Chapters 1-3 123

Preparation of Raw Data for Analysis and Tests of Assumptions 126

Preparation of Raw Data for Analysis 126

Tests of Assumptions 128

Descriptive Findings 145

Demographic Statistics 145

Results 158

Presenting the Results 158

Research Question One 159

Research Question Two 161

Research Question Three 162

Research Question Four 164

Research Question Five 166

Limitations 167

Summary 170

Chapter 5: Summary, Conclusions, and Recommendations 174

Introduction and Summary of Study 174

Summary of Findings and Conclusion 176

Overall Organization 176

Reflection on the Dissertation Process 190

Implications 191

    Theoretical Implications 191

    Practical Implications 192

    Future Implications 194

    Strengths and Weaknesses of the Study 195

Recommendations..197

    Recommendations for Future Research 197

    Recommendations for Future Practice..200

    Holistic Reflection on the Problem Space 201

List of Tables

Table 1.1 Alignment Table 9

Table 2.1 Description of Social Exchange Theory Costs and Benefits 18

Table 3.1 Variable Table - Predictors 67

Table 3.2 Variable Table - Criterion 68

Table 4.1 Updated Alignment Table 125

Table 4.2 Outliers by Variable 134

Table 4.3 Durbin-Watson Statistics 135

Table 4.4 Demographic Statistics – Age 145

Table 4.5 Demographic Statistics – State of Residence 146

Table 4.6 Demographic Statistics – Gender 147

Table 4.7 Demographic Statistics – Race 147

Table 4.8 Demographic Statistics – Length of Relationship 148

Table 4.9 Demographic Statistics – Education 149

Table 4.10 Demographic Statistics – Formal Mindfulness Training 150

Table 4.12 Reliability Statistics – Cronbach's Alpha 151

Table 4.13 Results of Data Analysis – Correlation Coefficient (Significance) 157

Table 4.14 Correlation Output – RQ1[a] 161

Table 4.15 Correlation Output – RQ3[a] 164

Table 4.16 Correlation Output – RQ4[a] 165

Table 4.17 Correlation Output – RQ5[a] 167

List of Figures

Figure 1 Scatterplots for Research Question One 129

Figure 2 Scatterplots for Research Question Two 130

Figure 3 Scatterplots for Research Question Three 131

Figure 4 Scatterplots for Research Question Four 132

Figure 5 Scatterplots for Research Question Five 133

Figure 6 P-P plots for RQ1 – Acting with Awareness 137

Figure 7 P-P plots for RQ2 - Observing 138

Figure 8 P-P plots for RQ3 - Describing 139

Figure 9 P-P plots for RQ4 – Non-judging 140

Figure 10 P-P plots for RQ5 – Non-reactivity 141

Chapter 1: Introduction to the Study

Introduction

Romantic relationships are central to the human experience and have been the focus of extensive academic inquiry. In contrast, mindfulness was popularized in the United States starting in the 1980s (Baer, 2019). Mindfulness in contemporary Western society is related to improving the holistic well-being of the individual; however, there is literature postulating the positive impact of mindfulness on romantic relationship well-being (Karremans et al., 2017). Conflict is an inherent part of any relationship. More importantly, conflict is implicated as a key predictor of relationship success or failure dependent upon the behavior exhibited by partners during a conflict interaction (Delatorre & Wagner, 2019). The behaviors displayed during conflict interactions are categorized into a set of conflict resolution and management strategies, more simply referred to as conflict strategies. There are presumptions in research that mindfulness benefits romantic relationships through increasing exhibition of helpful strategies and decreasing harmful strategies during conflict interactions; However, there is insufficient empirical evidence of a predictive relationship between the traits which make up mindfulness and the use of various romantic partner conflict strategies between adults in a committed romantic relationship.

The purpose of this quantitative predictive correlational study was to determine if and to what extent the five mechanisms of mindfulness identified in the Five Facet Mindfulness Questionnaire predict the six conflict strategy subdomains identified in the Romantic Partner Conflict Scale used by adults in a committed romantic relationship living in the mid-Atlantic region of the United States. The results of this study serve to support or refute the presumptions in existing literature that mindfulness positively predicts the use of desired conflict strategies while inversely predicting the use of harmful conflict strategies. Establishing empirical evidence of predictive relationships is a required precursor before conducting research to examine if mindfulness exists as a causal factor for conflict strategy use between adults in a committed romantic relationship.

If mindfulness is established as a predictor for romantic partner conflict strategy use, then an academic argument could be made to support the development of mindfulness programs as an intervention to improve romantic partner conflict interactions. There are a variety of existing therapeutic interventions for marital and romantic relationship improvement, so a practical application of this and subsequent research would be the integration of mindfulness principles in romantic partner therapy. This research is an extension of the very few existing studies which develop a foundation of empirical evidence to inform knowledge and practice surrounding mindfulness and romantic partnerships.

Background of the Study

Humans seek out pair-bonded, committed, and satisfactory relationships, but often romantic relationships are marred by harmful conflict resolution and management techniques. Harmful conflict strategies result in decreased relationship satisfaction and increased stress and stress-related problems (Shrout et al., 2020). Conflict is an inevitable part of any human relationship and is not inherently damaging. Nakonezny and Denton (2008) propose a valid method for improving relationship satisfaction is fostering positive interactions and decreasing negative interactions between partners. There is a highlighted need to understand factors associated with positive and negative romantic partner conflict interactions.

For decades mindfulness has been taught to increase personal well-being and emotion regulation. Mindfulness is the present-moment, non-judgmental awareness of experience (Kabat-Zinn, 2003). Mindfulness is a broad concept and includes a variety of cognitive processes, so for research and understanding, it is helpful to identify specific dimensions or traits. Trait mindfulness, as defined by Baer (2019), using Kabat-Zinn's model of mindfulness, identifies five specific dimensions of mindfulness: observing, describing, non-judging, acting with awareness, and non-reactivity. Due to the centrality of relationships in human functioning, it is essential to explore the relationship between mindfulness and interpersonal functioning.

This study was based on a call by Harvey et al. (2019) to study mindfulness and romantic partner conflict using a mindfulness tool that includes the non-judging facet of mindfulness. Featured heavily in Harvey et al. (2019), Karremans et al.(2017) is the publication a theory and model of potential mechanisms by which mindfulness benefits romantic relationships; however, the recommendation is that future research should explore empirical evidence to support or refute the theory.

The proposed research questions explore the predictive power of each identified facet of mindfulness for conflict strategy prevalence, which is compared against previous findings and provide new information related to the non-judging facet of mindfulness. This is accomplished through the use of the five-facet mindfulness questionnaire and the romantic partner conflict scale, both of which include distinct subscales. The previous research cited the mindfulness measure as a significant limitation which precluded the conclusion that mindfulness is an evidence-supported predictor variable for romantic partner conflict strategies. The current research builds on this previous evidence and to either support or refute mindfulness as a predictor of romantic partner conflict strategies. If mindfulness is supported as a predictor, then future research could conduct experimental studies to explore the efficacy of mindfulness interventions to improve romantic relationship conflict interactions and overall relationship functioning.

Definition of Terms

The following terms were used operationally in this study:

Adult. A person over 18 years of age (Canêo & Neirotti, 2017).

Committed. To be invested in the maintenance of a long-term relationship and having a sense of loyalty and dedication. The desire to maintain a romantic relationship over time (Gonzalez Avilés et al., 2021).

Conflict. Any situation where disagreement arises. Often, though not always, accompanied by angry, defensive, and/or hostile thoughts, feelings, and behaviors. A state of disharmony between two or more people regarding necessary action for resolution (Chavannes, 1898, p. 79).

Conflict Strategy Subdomains. The method by which individuals attempt to manage or resolve a conflict situation. The subdomains (e.g., compromising, dominating, submission) are identified based on the behaviors exhibited during the conflict interaction. Conflict strategy subdomains are generally distinguished based on the dimensions of constructive versus destructive and activity versus passivity (Mandal & Lip, 2022).

FFMQ. Five Facet Mindfulness Questionnaire. A 39-item self-report questionnaire used to measure an individual's trait mindfulness levels. First published by Baer et al. in 2006. This study uses the validated 15-item short form published by Baer et al. in 2008.

MBSR. Mindfulness-Based Stress Reduction. An 8-week course developed and run by Jon Kabat-Zinn using traditional Buddhist mindfulness practices and pioneering the use of mindfulness in the United States. The MBSR program was developed for the purpose of bringing traditional mindfulness into mainstream settings (Kabat-Zinn, 2011).

Mindfulness. An English translation of the Sanskrit word smrti. "The awareness that emerges through paying attention on purpose, in the present moment, and nonjudgmentally to the unfolding of experience moment by moment" (Kabat-Zinn, 2003, p. 145).

Social Exchange Theory. A conceptualization of human interaction in terms of losses and rewards. First published by Albert Chavannes in 1898. The belief that a successful society is predicated on interactions that are unanimously perceived as beneficial (Chavannes, 1898)

Trait Mindfulness. Sometimes referred to as dispositional mindfulness, it is the conceptualization of mindfulness as a set of practicable skills. According to Baer et al. (2006), the traits are observing, describing, acting with awareness, nonjudgmental acceptance of inner experiences, and non-reactivity to internal experiences.

Romantic Partner. Any person who identifies as being in a committed and sexual relationship. Marked by strong emotional, physical, and sexual attraction (Liebers, 2022).

RPCS. Romantic Partner Conflict Scale. A 39-item self-report questionnaire used to measure the presence of six conflict strategies used by romantic partners during typical, day to day conflict. First published in Zacchilli et al. (2009).

State Mindfulness. In contrast to trait mindfulness, it is the conceptualization of mindfulness as a state of being. A mind-state of being aware of each arising sensation to create harmony in the flow of energy (Sakuta, 2018).

Anticipated Limitations

Limitations are aspects of a study which reduce the validity and reliability of the findings and may be outside the researcher's control. This is not an exclusive list of factors affecting validity and reliability, and many others can be found in the assumptions and delimitations section of Chapter 3. The following limitations were anticipated given the study parameters:

- Data source limitations.

- Response bias. The study used self-report measures which are subject to inaccurate responses by participants. There is no independent verification of accurate responses. Self-report measures enable low-cost and anonymous data collection; however, responses may be biased by the participant's desire to provide 'the right' or most desirable answer or by lack of personal insight (Rosenman et al., 2011).

- Participant data. Confidence in accurately detecting significant results is dependent, in large part, on sample size. The required sample size was set at 98 participants based on an a priori power analysis using G*Power (Appendix F) which projected an appropriate effect size for avoiding Type II (false negative) error 80% of the time.

- Sampling limitations.

- Convenience sampling. Individuals were recruited for the study using snowball sampling via social media and may be inherently different from other adults in the target population. Additionally, individuals who volunteered to respond to the survey may be different from those who saw the post but did not participate. This limits the generalizability of the results (Salkind, 2010).

- Impact of COVID-19. The recent COVID-19 pandemic may affect participants' baseline personal and relational well-being which may impact the results of this study.

Summary and Organization of the Remainder of the Study

The primary purpose of the first chapter is to provide a background and overview of the study including potential limitations. A significant body of literature exists related to romantic relationships. This literature indicates that conflict interactions are particularly important for personal and relational health and functioning. Behaviors during conflict interactions are categorized as different conflict resolution and management strategies (e.g., compromising, dominating, avoidance, etc.). Some of these strategies are associated with relationship benefits while others are associated with negative personal and relational outcomes. Existing literature implicates mindfulness as a predictor of romantic conflict strategy prevalence; however, currently there is insufficient evidence to support that claim. The study has some anticipated limitations including the impact of COVID-19, the use of self-report data, and the use of convenience sampling. This concludes the introduction section, and the remaining sections detail the conceptual and methodological facets of the study.

The remaining chapters of this study are the literature review; methodology; data analysis and results; and summary, conclusions, and recommendations. The literature review includes a detailed discussion of the problem space, theoretical foundation, overview and synthesis of relevant literature, and the problem statement. The methodology chapter outlines the full proposed data collection and analysis procedures. Data analysis and results details the actual process of using the collected data to test the research hypotheses. This section includes any methodological changes to those proposed in Chapter 3. The summary, conclusions, and recommendations chapter is a narrative of the results from the data analysis within the context of existing literature as well as the implications for research and practice.

Feasibility refers to the practicality of a study. Feasibility includes participant access, the ability to recruit sufficient participants, and cost. Additional information regarding participant access, feasibility, and benefits is located in Appendix G. There are no ethical participant access concerns as the target population is not a closed, vulnerable, or protected class; however, recruitment could pose a challenge to feasibility as it may be difficult to find 98 adults willing to complete the study questionnaire. To avoid this recruitment challenge, the recruitment post was distributed to a pool of approximately 50,000 potential participants. Potential participants are accessed through approved Facebook pages (see Appendix B) and the researcher's personal page. Participant recruitment is not anticipated to create a barrier based on inclusion criteria as the only criteria for inclusion are age (over 18), location (mid-Atlantic US), and relationship status (committed romantic relationship). Mid-Atlantic US is defined as Maryland, Delaware, Pennsylvania, West Virginia, and Virginia based on the definition in a joint work between the Mid-Atlantic Regional Water Program and the US Department of Agriculture (Mid-Atlantic Water Program, 2006). Cost is not an anticipated barrier to feasibility as participants will be recruited using a free social media platform and no incentives are offered. There are no aspects of the study which pose a significant risk to feasibility.

Table 1.1

Alignment Table

Alignment Item	Alignment Item Description
Problem Space Need:	Conflict is implicated as a key predictor of relationship success or failure (Delatorre & Wagner, 2019). There are many points of convergence to suggest that mindfulness and romantic partner conflict behavior operate using shared mechanisms such as stress, emotion regulation, and non-judgement.
Problem Statement:	It was not known if and to what extent the five mechanisms of mindfulness identified in the Five Facet Mindfulness Questionnaire predict the six conflict strategy subdomains identified in the Romantic Partner Conflict Scale used by adults in a committed romantic relationship.
Purpose of the Study:	The purpose of this quantitative predictive correlational study was to determine if and to what extent the five mechanisms of mindfulness identified in the Five Facet Mindfulness Questionnaire predict the six conflict strategy subdomains identified in the Romantic Partner Conflict Scale used by adults in a committed romantic relationship living in the mid-Atlantic region of the United States.
Variables:	Mindfulness (identified as acting with awareness, observing, describing, non-reactivity, and non-judging by the FFMQ) measured at the individual level; Romantic partner conflict strategy subdomains (identified as compromising, domination, submission, avoidance, separation, and interactional reactivity by the RPCS) measured at the individual level.
Research Questions:	RQ1: Does **acting with awareness** predict **conflict strategy** subdomains used between adults in a committed romantic relationship? RQ2: Does **observing** predict **conflict strategy** subdomains used between adults in a committed romantic relationship? RQ3: Does **describing** predict **conflict strategy** subdomains used between adults in a committed romantic relationship? RQ4: Does **non-judging** predict **conflict strategy** subdomains used between adults in a committed romantic relationship? RQ5: Does **non-reactivity** predict **conflict strategy** subdomains used between adults in a committed romantic relationship?
Methodology/Research Design:	Quantitative Predictive Correlational

Chapter 2: Literature Review

Introduction to the Chapter and Background to the Problem

The following chapter provides a thorough examination of academic literature related to mindfulness, defined as the five traits in the Five Facet Mindfulness Questionnaire (Baer et al., 2006) and romantic relationships (general themes and conflict interactions). For each concept, this review includes a guiding theory, themes in the literature, changes in understanding and methodology over time, and areas requiring further academic exploration. First, analysis of current research highlights the problem space through the synthesis of research questions, methodology, limitations, and recommendations. This provides a foundation to guide the discussion of a theoretical framework. There is one theory identified for each discrete concept. Following the discussion of the guiding theories is a detailed exploration of themes and research related to each concept. The last section in the review of literature is a discussion of overlapping themes which creates an academic argument supporting the need for the proposed research. The research study is proposed in the problem statement which is the last section of this chapter.

The included and reviewed literature is the product of a thorough exploration including multiple databases and an exhaustive list of search terms. Primary search engines were the GCU online library with over 240 databases and Google Scholar. The most commonly used databases include DOAJ (Directory of Open Access Journals), SAGE Premier, Taylor & Francis, and JSTOR (Journal Storage). The search terms for mindfulness included: *mindfulness, Buddhism, Tao, Zen, Jon Kabat-Zinn, Thich Nhat Hanh, Smrti, traditional, contemporary, mindfulness theories, mindfulness* and *psychology, psychological theories of mindfulness, Mindfulness-Based Stress Reduction, Dialectical Behavior Therapy, Acceptance and Commitment Therapy, Mindfulness-Based Cognitive Therapy, Third-Wave Psychological therapies, Marsha Linehan, Ruth Ann Baer, Trait Mindfulness, Five-Facet Mindfulness Questionnaire, State Mindfulness, meditation, present, awareness, compassion,* and *mindfulness and negative outcomes.*

Search terms related to romantic partner conflict included: *romantic partners, intimate partners, marriage, marital, couples, cohabitation, interpersonal effectiveness, couple's therapy, Gottman, conflict, conflict resolution, conflict management, negative social behaviors, prosocial behaviors, culture, normative behavior, attachment theory, social exchange theory, wellness, well-being, mental health, communication styles, coregulation, emotional regulation, stress, protective factors, risk factors, intimacy,* and *connection.* Primarily, journal articles included in the review were published during or after 2017 unless they are from seminal authors, mark a pivotal change in conceptualization or methodology, or are particularly relevant to the proposed research study. For both featured variables (romantic relationships and mindfulness), compilation and synthesis revealed prevailing themes. Themes were developed based on existing understanding of the most important dimensions of each variable and for ease of reader understanding.

Background

Romantic partner functioning has been the topic of extensive academic research since the beginning of psychological research; however, mindfulness is a relatively new concept in Western academia. Kabat-Zinn (2011) specifically cites the desire to integrate traditional mindfulness into mainstream settings as a motivation for starting the

Mindfulness-Based Stress Reduction clinic. The changing landscape of mindfulness research is best demonstrated through the number of published articles. There were 0 published journal articles on mindfulness in 1980, but by 2016 there were 690 published journal articles studying mindfulness (Baer, 2019). Common areas of research related to mindfulness include traditional Buddhist roots (Dawson, 2021; Pemaratana & Khong, 2021), Stress, stress reduction, and physical health (e.g., Alsubaie et al., 2017; Cillessen et al., 2019; O'Loughlin et al., 2019), and Mindfulness-based psychological interventions (e.g., Dolbier et al., 2021; Mitchell et al., 2019; Rosales & Tan, 2017). The historical evolution of mindfulness in academic research is evidenced through both the number of academic publications per year and the expansion in the scope and recognized applicability of mindfulness.

Historically a prevalent topic in research, the timeline of romantic relationship research features changes in definitions, inclusivity, and purpose. Romantic partner research evolved from studying only heterosexual, cis-gender, monogamous, married couples to exploring diversity in the form and function of romantic relationships (Haas & Lannutti, 2021). Academics and policymakers also use research to illustrate societal problems and support reform. The social justice dynamic of romantic relationship research is demonstrated in publications such as Pereira et al. (2020) and Ogbuabor et al. (2021) which focus on intimate partner violence. Romantic partner research also has a strong tradition of exploring evidence-based interventions for improving romantic relationship functioning (maintenance and satisfaction, primarily). The sheer body of research on romantic partner conflict highlights the importance of conflict in relationship functioning (e.g., Delatorre & Wagner, 2019; Kim et al., 2007; Slatcher & Schoebi,

2017). The existing empirical research on romantic partner relationships changed over time to become more inclusive, highlight societal problems, and indicate conflict as an important facet of romantic partner functioning.

Modern academics have a foundation of research providing an understanding of the importance of relationship quality for personal and social functioning; however, there is still a need to develop effective interventions for improving the functioning of romantic relationships. Conflict has emerged as a prominent theme in relationship research, so it follows that research should focus on conflict as a target area for interventions to improve overall relationship functioning. There already exists theoretical literature and a few empirical studies which link mindfulness and romantic partner conflict; however, there is insufficient empirical evidence exploring a predictive relationship between mindfulness and romantic partner conflict strategies (Harvey et al., 2019). This is a necessary first step before considering mindfulness as an intervention to improve conflict in romantic relationships.

Identification of the Problem Space

This section demonstrates the need for the study based on recent empirical literature. Historically, romantic relationship research highlights the benefits of positive conflict interactions and the detriments of negative conflict interactions; however, there is still a need to identify ways of increasing positive conflict strategies and decreasing negative conflict strategies. Delatorre and Wagner (2019) published the conclusion that constructive conflict strategies are associated with lower divorce rates and increased relationship satisfaction. Poorly managed stress reactions are a primary cause of harmful conflict strategies. Losing self-control, anger, and defensiveness are all associated with reduced conflict resolutions (Staats et al., 2017). Over the last 40 years, mindfulness has steadily grown in academic popularity including the establishment of mindfulness as an effective stress management strategy. The majority of mindfulness research is focused on individual well-being, mostly stress management (O'Loughlin et al., 2019). Within the last five years, a new trend has emerged wherein mindfulness is studied for prosocial and interpersonal benefits. One example of this is Tekel and Erus (2020) which is a study demonstrating that mindfulness improves teachers' ability to interact positively with students even with high perceived stress levels. The trend toward identifying strategies for improving romantic partner conflict alongside the exploration of interpersonal mindfulness benefits led researchers to conduct studies exploring the relationship between mindfulness and romantic partner conflict interactions.

Several empirical studies have featured both mindfulness and romantic partner conflict as topics of interest. Harvey et al. (2019) is a quantitative predictive correlational study exploring whether mindfulness is a predictor for romantic partner conflict. The results of the study indicated that mindfulness is a predictor of compromise, interactional reactivity, and domination; however, cited limitations related to the mindfulness measure preclude the conclusion that mindfulness predicts conflict strategies. Mindfulness is also implicated as a predictor of conflict interactions in an older study published by the same researchers, and in that study, the mindfulness measure is also cited as a primary limitation because key aspects of mindfulness are not included (Harvey et al., 2015). Additionally, Quickert and MacDonald (2020) conducted a quantitative correlational study with 360 participants to investigate if mindfulness and rumination mediate the relationship between attachment insecurity and negative relationship conflict behaviors.

The results indicate that mindfulness mediates to decrease negative conflict behaviors while rumination mediates to increase them. These three studies collectively support mindfulness as a predictor of romantic conflict strategies; however, limitations based on measurement tools decrease the validity of the findings and call in to question whether or not mindfulness is actually an evidence-based predictor of romantic partner conflict strategies.

This existing empirical evidence supports current theoretical models related to mindfulness and romantic partner functioning. Featured heavily in Harvey et al. (2019), Karremans et al. (2017) is the publication of a theoretical model for a variety of possible ways that mindfulness could benefit romantic relationships with the recommendation that empirical research should explore the specific mechanisms of mindfulness responsible for romantic relationship benefits. The theoretical model published in 2017 became the basis for empirical studies published thereafter including Harvey et al. (2019) and Mandal and Lip (2022) which demonstrated partial support for mindfulness as predictor of conflict strategies based on the individual mechanisms, or dimensions, of mindfulness. The trend in recent literature related to mindfulness and romantic partner conflict strategies highlights the importance of discussing mindfulness in terms of facets rather than as an overarching concept. The cited limitation of insufficient mindfulness measures to capture all the identified facets of mindfulness support the need to explore if and to what extent the five mechanisms of mindfulness identified in the five-facet mindfulness questionnaire predict the six conflict strategy subdomains identified in the Romantic Partner Conflict Scale used by adults in a committed romantic relationship.

It is essential to establish a valid and unequivocal foundation of correlative research to justify the resources needed to conduct a rigorous experimental study. Rigorous experimental studies are costly in terms of time, money, and effort, yet they are necessary to develop new evidence-based treatment interventions in addition to increasing the body of academic knowledge. While it is possible to establish a predictive relationship without an experiment, only rigorous experimental studies are able to determine a causal relationship (Lobmeier, 2010). This study is a continuation of the current research trend to explore the social benefits of mindfulness specifically related to improving romantic partner conflict. This research will add to the body of research in both areas. The study will serve to establish a solid research base from which to recommend dedication of resources for rigorous experimental studies. Experimental studies would be the foundation for concluding that mindfulness has a causal relationship with romantic partner conflict strategy use. This would support the development of an evidence-based mindfulness-based intervention to improve romantic partner functioning. Healthy conflict resolution is a longstanding target of romantic relationship therapy, so the addition of a new evidence-based intervention would be profound. This study is a necessary link in the chain from theory through research to practical application.

Theoretical Foundations

Social Exchange Theory

Social exchange theory explains human interaction as a system of costs and benefits. The first academic mention of social exchange is by Albert Chavannes, a sociologist, in the late 19th century. Even in this first mention Chavannes (1898 p. 59) defines social exchange in terms of money and goods and also as it relates to affection and enjoyment of one another. In a series of publications Chavannes lays out his law of exchange, nature of the mind, and law of conduct. The earliest proponent of social exchange theory, Chavannes posits that exchange which is unanimously regarded as positive is the foundation of a successful society (Chavannes, 1898). Although Chavannes published the earliest mention of social exchange, academic literature exists which credits others for the develop of social exchange theory.

Despite Albert Chavannes' publication of the law of exchange in 1898, many regard George Homans as the founder of social exchange theory. Homans published two notable papers on social exchange in 1958 and 1961 (Nord, 1973). However, by this time there were already several publications on the principles of social exchange as it relates to romantic and marital relationships as cited in Nakonezny and Denton (2008). Using the lens of social exchange theory, the costs and benefits experienced during couples' interactions account for romantic relationship processes. Each interaction between the partners is labeled as either positive or negative and of variable worth. Greater instances of highly valued positive interactions are associated with increased satisfaction and commitment to the relationship (Nakonezny & Denton, 2008). One criticism of social exchange theory is the lack of consistency between cost/benefit appraisals and value (see table 2.1).

Table 2.1

Description of Social Exchange Theory Costs and Benefits

Types of Exchanges	Definition of the Exchange	Examples of the Exchange
Profitable/ Positive	The party receives their desired outcome with negligible costs.	Attention Affection Support Gifts
Costly/ Negative	The exchange results in a loss to the party. The party does not achieve the desired outcome, or the cost is greater than the benefit.	Time Effort Status Stress Emotional Distress

There are some notable criticisms and limitations of social exchange theory. A primary criticism from Blau (1964) cites the inconsistent labeling of an exchange as positive or negative and the variable worth of those exchanges. Essentially, one person may view dinner with the mother-in-law as a benefit of the romantic relationship while another person views it as a cost. Even if both people view the exchange as either positive or negative, the value of that exchange will almost always vary from person to person. These inconsistencies make it impossible to unequivocally categorize costs and benefits. Another major criticism is the post hoc nature by which people appraise their social exchanges (Bem, 1972). This means that many times people appraise an interaction after it takes place using the consequences and actual emotional experience. This also serves to make predictions impossible which is a limitation to the practical use of social exchange theory. Perhaps even more challenging is the inability or unwillingness of couples to communicate their appraisals of various exchanges (Nakonezny & Denton, 2008, p. 410). While these limitations are valid, social exchange theory continues to be the basis for some of the most widely used therapeutic interventions and research measuring tools.

Social exchange theory has been adapted over the years and served as the foundation for numerous therapies and measurement tools which are used in contemporary clinical practice and research. Solution-focused therapy and emotion-focused therapy are two of the most well-known therapies which have their foundation in social exchange theory (Nakonezny & Denton, 2008). Both therapies are designed to work with individuals to minimize costs and maximize rewards. The Gottmans are renowned researchers and therapists specializing in romantic partner relationships and a major tenet of their work is increasing the ratio of positive to negative encounters in a relationship (Gottman & Levenson, 1992). Social Exchange theory is also one of the foundations for the romantic partner conflict scale which measures positive, negative, and uncategorized behaviors exhibited by romantic partners during a conflict interaction (Zacchilli et al., 2009). Conflict is an inherent part of any social relationship and the ability to manage conflict positively would naturally increase the positive exchanges while decreasing the negative exchanges in the relationship.

Kabat-Zinn's Model of Mindfulness

Mindfulness is a historically Buddhist concept which has recently entered academic and clinical use in Western society. The word mindfulness is the English translation of the Sanskrit word, Smrti which is 'bare attention' or even 'memory' (Garcia-Campayo et al., 2021). Bare attention in this context means observation without adding mental stories or creating a meaning for what is perceived. Traditionally mindfulness is a practice of bringing one's attention to some aspect of the present moment in a nonjudgmental way (See Figure 2; Kabat-Zinn, 2003). One may bring attention to a particular feeling, such as anger or jealousy, without adding a mental story that it is unacceptable to have the feeling. Kabat-Zinn (2003) notes that Buddhists have been practicing the art of mindfulness and mindful meditation for over 2,500 years; however, mindfulness only recently received popularity in the United States. In 1980 there were no published journal articles on mindfulness, but in 2016 there were 690 published journal articles (Baer, 2019). This contemporary popularization includes use of mindfulness principles and practices in a variety of research and clinical settings.

Jon Kabat-Zinn popularized the use of mindfulness as a clinical and research topic of interest. Using the mindfulness meditation and yoga traditions of Hindu, Buddhist, and Zen traditions, Kabat-Zinn started the mindfulness-based stress reduction (MBSR) clinic in 1979 (Kabat-Zinn, 2011). At that time, it was named the stress reduction and relaxation program. MBSR is an 8-week program which has evidence supporting its effectiveness for reducing stress and symptoms associated with various medical and mental health conditions (Juul et al., 2018). Kabat-Zinn's model and philosophy of mindfulness also influenced the development of Marsha Linehan's mindfulness dimension in dialectical behavior therapy (DBT) (Baer, 2019). DBT is the prevailing treatment for borderline personality disorder, suicidal patients, substance use disorders, and more (Robins et al., 2010, p. 53). DBT features mindfulness as one of four primary modules of skill development. In modern Western clinical culture, mindfulness is not just one skill but rather a multi-faceted concept which parallels the traditional Eastern conceptualization.

Mindfulness is a dynamic and richly traditional concept. Researchers have developed numerous tools to try to capture an individual's level of mindfulness by self-report of certain traits. The tool which most closely aligns with the work of Jon Kabat-Zinn's model of mindfulness is the five-facet mindfulness questionnaire (FFMQ). The five facets or traits of mindfulness according to the FFMQ are: observing, describing, non-judging, acting with awareness, and non-reactivity (Baer et al., 2006). The FFMQ is used in a variety of current empirical studies including Moix et al. (2021) in which the FFMQ was administered to measure changes in mindfulness by self-reporting associated with a brief training and experience of anxiety symptoms. The model of mindfulness developed by Jon Kabat-Zinn is the bridge from traditional Buddhist mindfulness to the foundation of contemporary clinical and research use.

Review of the Literature

The literature review is organized by broad research category (romantic relationships and mindfulness) then further developed into primary themes from current and relevant literature identifying specific variables for use in the study. Themes in romantic relationships include: the influence of culture, the reciprocity of personal and relational well-being, attempts to predict long-term success, and the centrality of conflict in a relationship. Themes in mindfulness research are traditional, contemporary, and the rise of trait and dispositional mindfulness. Points of convergence are discussed which identify overlapping themes between mindfulness and romantic relationship research which serve to highlight the practicality of exploring a quantifiable predictive relationship between the two.

Couples in a Romantic Relationship

Throughout time and place humans have sought out romantic partnerships. Typically, romantic relationships are characterized by exclusive sexual intimacy and commitment which is the desire to maintain the relationship for a long time (Gonzalez Avilés et al., 2021). Adolescents and adults seek out relationships because it is part of their cultural life script (Hoplock & Stinson, 2021), to meet physical needs such as procreation and physical intimacy, and to meet emotional needs like social support and loneliness prevention (Kansky, 2018). This variety of benefits is available to individuals in romantic relationships but is not guaranteed simply by being in a romantic relationship. The availability of benefits to the individuals in the romantic partnership is determined by a blend of cultural, individual, and relational factors. The potential for high reward or severe detriment combined with the probability that most people will be in a romantic relationship at some point in their life necessitates the exploration of factors influencing relationship experience and maintenance.

Variation by Culture. Romantic relationships vary by culture. Culture is a complex, pervasive, multi-dimensional concept. Culture can be defined as both the external reality such as cities and artifacts as well as the internal reality of individuals and their communities (Mironenko & Sorokin, 2018). For the purposes of this literature review, discussion of culture will be limited to form, function, gender-normed behavior, and deviant behavior in the form of intimate partner violence. In many areas, developing and maintaining a romantic relationship is an expected part of development during late adolescence and early adulthood (Hoplock & Stinson, 2021). With variation in culture comes variation in accepted form and expected function of romantic relationships. It is important to recognize the influence of culture on the individual and therefore the relationship prior to attempting to analyze problem areas or potential solutions.

Relationship form refers to a variety of types of relationships, including monogamous, polyamorous, homosexual, heterosexual, and bisexual. LGBTQIA+ is a term referring to all sexual relationships that are not cis gender (gender identity/expression matches gender assigned at birth), heterosexual, and monogamous. Research suggests that relationship maintenance behaviors are the same across minority and majority sexual relationships except for negotiation and willingness to engage in shared tasks which is a less important behavior in LGBTQIA+ relationships perhaps due to assumptions of role equality and flexibility (Haas & Lannutti, 2021). The majority of research on romantic relationships has focused on the majority relationship form which is cis-gender, monogamous and heterosexual although emerging research explores similarities and differences between majority and minority relationship forms. Research findings indicate negative relationship outcomes associated with anxious and avoidant attachment styles in polyamorous relationships (Moors et al., 2019) just as in monogamous relationships (Park et al., 2019). These results indicate that while there are similarities across all romantic relationships in terms of attachment orientation and relationship maintenance behaviors, there may be inherent differences as a result of identifying as part of a sexual minority group.

Another type of relationship form is often associated with commitment and includes labels such as dating, cohabitating, and married. In Western cultures there is an accepted life script popularized by the nursery rhyme, 'first comes love, then comes marriage, then comes baby in the baby carriage' which highlights the expectation that individuals will meet, marry, and procreate in that order (Hoplock & Stinson, 2021). A cultural life script prescribes events and timing in an accepted range which inherently marks anything outside to be unacceptable and possibly stigmatizing. The rise of cohabitation has drastically increased the complexity of romantic relationship research because cohabitation varies in form from short-term, non-committal cohabitation to being essentially a parallel of a marital relationship (Sassler & Lichter, 2020). While cohabitation is a violation of traditional Western cultural norms, its increasing prevalence has sparked research into the similarities and differences between long-term committed cohabitation and marriage. Marriage rates have declined with the rise of cohabitation (Sassler & Lichter, 2020); however, relationship satisfaction may still be higher for married versus cohabitating partners (Braithwaite & Holt-Lunstad, 2017). Cultural norms related to relationship forms are changing, but the function of these relationships remains the same.

Regardless of form, romantic relationships fulfill individual and societal needs and therefore have a function. Establishing and maintaining a romantic relationship is a critical psychosocial task which affects a person's identity (Kansky & Allen, 2018). Therefore, a key function of being in a romantic relationship is related to an individual's ability to conform to pervasive societal norms and avoid social stigma associated with not being able to be in or stay in a romantic relationship. Many individuals enter their first romantic relationship sometime during adolescence and it provides an opportunity to acquire communication skills such as active listening and negotiating (Couture et al., 2021). While romantic relationships provide an opportunity for social support, intimacy, skill acquisition, procreation, personal and occupational fulfillment, financial support, and stress management, relationship dynamics and quality affect the ability of partners to experience these benefits. Romantic relationships provide the opportunity for emotional intimacy, but many are unable to experience this benefit because it requires a willingness to make oneself vulnerable and to forego self-protecting behaviors (Emery & Finkel, 2021). Romantic relationships can fulfill an array of basic human needs, but it is the quality of the relationship that determines its success at functionally meeting those needs.

Although recent years have seen a substantial shift, gender norms are still a pervasive force in romantic relationships. Typically, gender norms refer to unequal expectations (sexual double standards) or perceptions of differential traits (e.g., boys as tough and girls as weak; Ramaiya et al., 2021). Unequal expectations in a romantic relationship include expectations about sexual behavior, child rearing, financial roles, household chores, and so forth. These internalized social hierarchies in romantic relationships form early in adolescence and across a variety of cultural settings (Moreau et al., 2019). Traditional gender norms are not always beneficial to romantic relationships. Despite the norm that men should be work-oriented, women married to family-oriented men reported higher satisfaction with their lives and less work-family conflict (Meeussen et al., 2019). The benefit associated with being in relationships with people who do not conform to traditional gender stereotypes is a key component when considering the mechanisms for improving romantic relationship functioning.

Closely associated with traditional gender norms, intimate partner violence (IPV) is a changing cultural concept. Some aspects of culture most associated with IPV include cultures that approve of violence against women, those that attribute authority exclusively or predominantly to men, and those where familial and social support is not readily available to victims (Pereira et al., 2020). Unsurprisingly, IPV has clear effects on individual and relational well-being. Affecting both the victim and the perpetrator, IPV results in various biopsychosocial consequences including depression, posttraumatic stress disorder, difficulty with daily activities, memory loss, stress, suicidal thoughts and attempts, and even poor social outcomes for children who witness IPV (Ogbuabor et al., 2021). All of these negative effects of IPV reinforce that romantic relationships provide the opportunity for but are not a guarantee of benefits for the individuals who are in them.

Relationships and Wellbeing. Research on well-being includes both subjective and objective measures. Subjective measures include items such as self-report of positive emotions, energy, functioning, personal growth, purpose, autonomy, and self-acceptance (Pritchard et al., 2020). Definitions of well-being which use subjective measurements determine an individual's felt sense or perception of their own well-being while objective measures are observed by others. Objective measures of well-being include physical markers (absence or presence of disease, ability to performance daily living tasks, and Body Mass Index) and psychological measures (observed symptoms of mental disorders; Masciocchi et al., 2020). While subjective and objective measurements exist, there is not consensus among academics or professionals for how to operationalize definitions of well-being.

Operational definitions of well-being typically align with either eudaimonic or hedonic perspectives. An operationalized definition is one that proposes measurable characteristics to describe an abstract concept. Eudaimonism is a concept dating back to the Greek philosopher, Aristotle who suggested that well-being is comprised of living in accordance with one's true self, aligned with their values and having achieved their full potential (Pritchard et al., 2020). Each of these major tenets of eudaimonic well-being can be operationalized and measured for the purposes of psychological research, as can those associated with hedonic well-being. Hedonic well-being is rooted in the pursuit of pleasure and avoidance of pain (Twiselton et al., 2020). Hedonism suggests that well-being is directly related to the levels of positive emotion versus negative emotion that a person experiences. Current research suggests that the most accurate measurement of overall well-being is one that combines elements of eudaimonic and hedonic philosophy to achieve a full and balanced life experience (Twiselton et al., 2020). The importance of balancing pleasurable life experience, values, and fulfillment suggests that improving well-being must focus on more than simply increasing pleasurable emotions. This understanding of individual well-being allows for evidence-based discussion of the interconnected nature of individual and relational health.

Individual well-being and relationship health exist as inextricably and reciprocally connected. Healthy, supportive, and loving relationships are associated with higher rates of safety, self-esteem, life satisfaction, and achievement of goals while relationships with violence resulted in higher levels of anxiety, stress, depression, low self-esteem, and low life satisfaction for both victim and perpetrator (Gómez-López et al., 2019). Healthy romantic relationships facilitate personal well-being and unhealthy relationships put individuals at greater risk of experiencing problems. One model of the association between romantic relationships and mental health suggests that relationship quality, relationship stress, and adaptive/maladaptive processes moderate the effect of relationship status on a person's mental health (Braithwaite & Holt-Lunstad, 2017). Adaptive and maladaptive processes refer to the coping skills that the individuals in the relationship develop to manage relationship situations and stress. This evidence indicates that while normally being in a romantic relationship has a positive impact on one's mental health, when the relationship is dysfunctional then the romantic relationship harms one's mental health. While not a 1-to-1 correspondence, there is a predictive association between romantic relationship quality and individual well-being.

Healthy romantic relationships improve an individual's overall wellbeing. Characteristics of a healthy relationship include emotional intimacy, mutually beneficial sexual intimacy, trust, and social support (Kansky, 2018). Well-being refers not only to the previously discussed mental health benefits of a supportive romantic relationship, but also physical and social benefits. Physical benefits include longer life and lower prevalence of disorders, while social benefits are increased job satisfaction, job performance, and academic performance (Kansky, 2018). These benefits are not equal across all types of romantic relationships. Current literature suggests increased benefits associated with greater levels of intimacy, and married individuals are the most likely to experience the greatest personal benefits from their relationship (Braithwaite & Holt-Lunstad, 2017). Functional intimate relationships increase the biopsychosocial well-being of individuals, so it is important to identify the factors in addition to form and function which influences adult romantic relationships.

Other Noteworthy Influences. In addition to form, function, and association with wellness, a discussion of romantic relationships would be remiss without exploring the influences that are at the core of most romantic partnerships. Noteworthy influences on romantic relationships include the COVID-19 pandemic, sexual activity, social media use, finances, personal values, and trust. Each of these concepts emerged as a central theme in the area of romantic relationship research because each significantly impacts the health and functioning of the relationship.

The COVID-19 pandemic was an acute stressor with long-term effects which caused romantic partners to face never-before-seen challenges including extended quarantine and social isolation. One study noted that family dysfunction affected romantic partner intimacy and posits that the significant increase in stressors could be responsible for the dramatic increase in displayed family dysfunction and pose a risk for marital breakdown (Feng et al., 2021). Stressors during the COVID-19 pandemic include school closures, economic instability, confinement to living quarters, and fear of COVID-19 infection among other things. Intimate partner violence is another relationship-related COVID-19 impact which dramatically increased (23.38% in Spain) due to the forced lockdown and economic stress (Arenas-Arroyo et al., 2021).While it is clear that many couples suffered due to COVID-19, this may not be the case for all couples. Pietromonaco and Overall (2021) report that responses to COVID-19 mirror those to trauma in that some experience devastation while others experience resilience and growth. Given the demonstrated increase in violence, resilience, and other romantic relationship outcomes, it is essential to consider that COVID-19 is a significant influence on all psychological research from 2020 onward.

One of the primary identifying factors of a romantic relationship is that the partners are sexually intimate (although given religious beliefs, some may identify as being in a committed, romantic relationship even while they are not sexually active). Altgelt and Meltzer (2021) identified the frequency of sex and sexual satisfaction as two important determinants of marital satisfaction and dissolution. Using the analogy of the domino effect wherein one thing causes the next which causes the next and so on, it is critical to identify the factors which influence sexual frequency and satisfaction. There is evidence to suggest that engaging in post sex affection increases both sexual and relationship satisfaction (Muise et al., 2014). In addition to post sex affection, communication is also highly implicated as a fundamental determinant of sexual functioning in romantic relationships. Rubinsky et al. (2021) cites sexual communication as a predictor of communication satisfaction as well as relational and sexual satisfaction, and note that, despite the clear benefits of good sexual communication, many couples avoid sexual communication because it is vulnerable. Related to sexual communication, there is a widespread belief that sexual activity following conflict is the most pleasurable. However, evidence suggests that while sex that co-occurs on conflict days buffers the negative effects of conflict, the sexual experience itself is less pleasurable than on non-conflict days (Maxwell & Meltzer, 2020). Given this evidence, the sexual facet of a romantic relationship is both a cause and effect of various personal and relational dynamics.

Another determinant of personal and relational dynamics, the increasingly ubiquitous presence of cell phones necessitates the need to discuss the effect of cell phone and social media use on romantic relationships. Evidence suggests that social media use often escalates distress and conflict in a relationship (Fox et al., 2014), and photo manipulation behaviors on social media can lead to social media-induced infidelity and relationship dissolution (Stewart & Clayton, 2022). Regardless of social media activity, cell phone use of any sort impacts romantic relationship functioning. A qualitative research study indicated negative experiences related to a partner being on the phone when there was an expectation of having the partner's attention (Kelly et al., 2017). Thus, the negative emotional experiences were related to feelings of neglect or being ignored. The same research study also noted positive experiences when participants observed their partners using intention to reduce cell phone related distractions to prioritize quality time (see Kelly et al., 2017). While cell phone and social media have a strong potential for negative effects and experiences, partners can also use intention to demonstrate prioritizing time with their partner to help create positive experiences.

In modern society, money is an inescapable part of life which means that adult partners in a relationship must navigate finances and financial conversations. Differences in financial beliefs and approaches leads to financial conflict which is a predictor of marital dissatisfaction and divorce (LeBaron et al., 2019). Financial infidelity is one particularly detrimental behavior associated with mismanaged differences in financial attitudes. Financial infidelity is defined as intentionally hiding financial activity due to the expectation that a partner would be disapproving, and it has the potential to be as destructive to the romantic relationship as sexual infidelity (Garbinsky et al., 2020). The potential for equal destructiveness between sexual and financial infidelity suggests that finances are a critically important aspect of romantic relationship functioning. Perhaps, financial practices and discussions are important not because money is important but because the behavior and communication highlight the negative conflict patterns, feelings of inequity and unfairness, trigger stress associated with economic pressure (Kaittila, 2020). Therefore, it is likely that money itself may not always be important, but finances are an important determinant of relationship functioning as a symbol of underlying relational patterns and personal values.

In a relationship, an individual cedes some level of independence and control which requires trust in another person to maintain a sense of safety. Trust is one of the most important parts of a healthy and stable foundation for a romantic relationship (Campbell & Stanton, 2019). If the goal is to achieve a healthy and stable relationship, then individuals should select partners who present as trustworthy. Evidence supports that people select romantic partners who exhibit trustworthiness in favor of any other personality trait (Mogilski et al., 2019). Unfortunately, the level of trust is not solely determined by the integrity of the behaviors exhibited by partners in a current relationship. Individuals enter a relationship with experiences and beliefs which create a propensity for trust or mistrust (Campbell & Stanton, 2019). This implies that developing trust in a relationship may also require an individual to resolve betrayals of trust from earlier in life. Some behaviors that increase or restore trust include quality time, sexual intimacy, and receiving gifts from a partner (Matson et al., 2021). Current literature supports the primacy of trust provides a lens for understanding trust development which can foster overall relationship improvement.

Improving relationship quality is an evidence-based practice for improving the well-being of people in romantic relationships. While there is a predictive bi-directional association between relationships and mental health, a stronger causal effect occurs when mental health is the outcome and relationships are the predictor (Braithwaite & Holt-Lunstad, 2017). This suggests that relationship quality has a more direct impact on individual well-being than well-being has on relationship quality. Relationship quality is an important consideration beyond just relationship presence or absence as it relates to the association of relationships and well-being (Gómez-López et al., 2019). The importance of relationship functioning on individual well-being supports the need to identify factors in romantic relationships which determine their success or failure.

Predictors of Success. Romantic relationships are an integral part of adult life and factors associated with healthy and satisfying relationships have been the focus of a wide array of research. Predictors of success are relationship characteristics which are highly correlated with positive outcomes such as satisfaction, well-being, and long-term maintenance. According to Slatcher and Schoebi (2017), in a meta-analysis of marital processes indicative of beneficial health outcomes, two protective processes are partner responsiveness and emotion regulation. Some constructs such as satisfaction and commitment are discussed as either predictors or outcomes of successful relationships. Another primary theme in romantic relationship research is the conflict which is discussed as a predictor of either relationship success or failure. Similarly, each predictor of success can be reversed to be a predictor of failure. Due to the finding that relationship dissolution is more directly linked to loss of rewards than to accrual of costs (Nakonezny & Denton, 2008) characteristics associated with relationship success are highlighted.

Partner responsiveness is a predictor of a successful relationship. Partner responsiveness is also referred to as attunement which is the process of being attentive to another person and their needs (Slatcher & Schoebi, 2017). Attunement is both a cognitive and physiological process requiring certain skills and can be facilitated through specific activities. Physiological attunement as measured by heart rate indicated that poor coregulation is highly associated with negative affect and perceptions of the partner as cold (Schreiber et al., 2020). Partner responsiveness is a direct correlate to a social support need to be fulfilled by romantic relationships. Attunement is also directly related to other key needs in relationships such as belonging, trust, intimacy, secure attachments, and acceptance (Slatcher & Schoebi, 2017). These needs are met through consistent and caring responsiveness during a variety of normal relationship activities.

Partner responsiveness is the use of prosocial skills which improve the partners' experiences of inevitable relationship tasks. Partners who are attentive during conversation buffer stress and provide social support for their partners (Schreiber et al., 2020). The ability to dedicate sustained attention in a conversation requires awareness that attention is important and the ability to resist any impulses for distraction or multitasking. Activities which involve attunement include partner self-disclosures, participating in an activity together, discussing future goals, conflict, or planning an event (Slatcher & Schoebi, 2017). Warmth, caring, and acceptance conveyed during these activities increases personal positive affect and strengthen the trust and intimacy of the relationship. In attachment theory, secure attachments exist when individuals trust their partner (caregiver in early childhood then romantic partner in adulthood) to provide safety and comfort when needed or to support autonomy and exploration (Virat & Dubreil, 2020). The ability to attune to a partner and to receive a partner's responsiveness attempts requires the ability to emotionally regulate.

While seemingly an individual process, emotion regulation is a critical predictor of relationship success. Affective or emotional interdependence is inherent in close relationships and is both the potential for increased and sustained positive emotional experiences and the source of emotional vulnerability due to a lack of exclusive control over one's emotional state (Slatcher & Schoebi, 2017). Using the effects on relationship outcomes, Kim et al. (2007) established three tiers of affects as 1) positive; interest, validation, affection, humor, and enthusiasm; 2) low-intensity negative; domineering, whining, anger, fear/tension, and sadness; and 3) high-intensity negative; contempt, belligerence, and defensiveness. The presence or absence of these emotions during relationship interactions determines the ratio of positive to negative encounters which partly determines an individual's appraisal of the health of their relationship. Gottman and Levenson (1992) observed a couple's conflict interactions and identified couples as either regulated or nonregulated which predicted marital satisfaction, dissolution, and health outcomes. The ability to use emotion regulation as a predicting variable for relationship success supports its standing as a characteristic of great importance.

Discussed as both predictors and outcomes of successful relationships, satisfaction, commitment, and long-term maintenance emerged as pervasive themes in the current literature on adult romantic relationships. In Schreiber et al. (2020) long-term maintenance and relationship satisfaction were used as outcome measures of disrupted coregulation during conflict. However, satisfaction and commitment are both listed as marital strengths in the strength and strain model of relationship quality (Slatcher & Schoebi, 2017). Commitment and long-term maintenance are often discussed in tandem and are closely associated with satisfaction. The lack of clarity in the literature regarding the classification of these concepts as either predictors or outcomes prohibits their further discussion.

Conflict Strategies

The final pervasive theme in the literature on the quality of romantic relationships is conflict. Conflict is an inherent part of any relationship between two people (Zacchilli et al., 2009) and can be defined simply as an area of disagreement (Schreiber et al.,

2020). The seminal author of Social Exchange Theory identifies people as being in conflict when "they are not in harmony with the line of conduct which must be followed to work out the potentialities which exist" (Chavannes, 1898, p.79). Naturally, the intensity, duration, emotions, and behaviors will all vary. Conflict is often associated with hostility and related processes but can also be an example of partner responsiveness when the conflict situation is perceived as having gone well (Slatcher & Schoebi, 2017). A thorough discussion of conflict highlights underlying themes such as attachment, family and cultural influences, resolution styles, emotion regulation, biology, and reconciliation processes. The endemic nature of conflict combined with the potential for deleterious or beneficial effects marks conflict as an important topic in the field of romantic relationships.

Research on interpersonal conflict categorized a variety of resolution and management strategies. These strategies are characterized by observable behaviors and are classified as positive problem-solving (compromise), conflict engagement (defensive and/or attacking), and withdrawal (refusal to participate; Staats et al., 2017). Some research suggests that collaborative, argumentative, and disengaging are not sufficient to cover the wide array of conflict behaviors. A fourth management style is compliance which is characterized by not defending one's position and easily giving in to the other party (Ha et al., 2012). Any single conflict interaction can have elements of different management styles, both because individuals can exhibit behaviors from multiple styles (one person, many behaviors) and because each individual will have a unique responding style (multiple people means multiple behaviors). However, relationships with constructive conflict strategies are associated with lower rates of divorce and increased relationship satisfaction (Delatorre & Wagner, 2019). The strong association between conflict style and relationship quality indicates a need to understand the factors which contribute to individual and relational conflict behaviors.

As with partner responsiveness, the ability to engage in productive conflict resolution requires emotion regulation. Individuals experiencing anxiety are less positive during conflict which tends to escalate the conflict situation (Petersen & Le, 2017). Negative conflict behaviors are associated with identifiable and predictable emotional responses. Losing self-control, anger, defensiveness (Staats et al., 2017) and attempting to inhibit or conceal emotional expression (Thomson et al., 2018) are all associated with low conflict resolution. Another psychological influence, self-esteem and conflict management exist in a reciprocal relationship. Poor self-esteem results in psychological distress which is associated with negative mood, and the distress and negative mood then escalate each other (Petersen & Le, 2017). The ability to regulate negative emotions and resist the impulse to act on them is a key aspect of functioning in a conflict situation. Emotion regulation during conflict situations is sometimes measured as one's ability to adaptively engage in conflict using cognitive reappraisal which is the ability to change how one thinks about a situation to minimize emotional impact (Low et al., 2019). The behaviors associated with functional conflict resolution inherently require the regulation of emotions and emotional impulses so that they are able to remain grounded and rational enough to engage in collaboration, empathy, and cognitive reappraisal.

Attachment, secure versus insecure, often presents as a significant factor affecting the processes and outcomes of romantic partner conflict. One type of insecure attachment is an anxious attachment wherein a partner has excessive need for approval and experiences distress if their partner is unavailable or unresponsive (Paquette et al., 2020). On the other end of the spectrum is avoidant attachment. Avoidant attachment, also classified as insecure, is characterized by fear of dependence, reluctance to self-disclose or become intimate, and excessive need for self-reliance (Paquette et al., 2020). Secure attachment exists as a functional balance between self-reliance and codependence, which has implications for conflict management and resolution. Secure attachment style is associated with a greater presence of mutually focused conflict styles such as positive problem solving (Petersen & Le, 2017), appropriate management of negative affect (Bonache et al., 2017), and constructive engagement during conflict situations (Feeney & Karantzas, 2017). Attachment theory not only categorizes and explains variation in relationship functioning, but also provides a direct theoretical link to the influence of family on adult romantic relationships.

Family is typically the formative environment for all individuals, so it follows that family and cultural norms will influence the strategies used by an individual to manage or resolve conflicts. Cultural norms can lead to irrational beliefs, such as 'disagreement is destructive', which can result in unhelpful emotions and behaviors including increased use of harmful conflict management styles (Aušraitė & Žardeckaitė-Matulaitienė, 2019). This example highlights the direct process from the cultural norm through internalized belief to the behavioral response. Traditional masculinity, a gender norm and cultural value, is linked with the more frequent use of destructive conflict styles and less frequent use of constructive conflict resolution strategies (Rogers et al., 2020). Culture and family influence individuals' value systems which are closely tied to an individual's identity. When a conflict involves a core value (e.g., honesty, reliability, loyalty), parties are both more likely to view the conflict as more negative and less likely to reach a satisfying resolution for either party (Schuster et al., 2020). Recall that financial conflict causes significant problems for romantic partners, perhaps due to the connection with a variety of personal values. The family system is primarily responsible for the development of attachment styles, behavior norms, and values all of which strongly influence the perception of and interaction during romantic partner conflicts.

    Several biological markers directly correlate to various aspects of conflict which facilitates the objective measurement of conflict dynamics. Oxytocin, associated with a variety of relational, sexual, and emotional processes, is associated with validating, or understanding behavior during a sexual conflict discussion (Roels et al., 2021). This indicates a direct link between neurohormonal functioning and romantic partner sexual communications. Used as measures of stress, cardiovascular response and cortisol patterns reveal links between physiological stress responses and conflict behaviors. A study involving veterans with PTSD and their spouses demonstrated a connection between cardiovascular reactivity (physical stress response) and harmful relationship conflict behaviors (Smith et al., 2021). The connection between physiological stress and negative behaviors is maintained when using alternative measures of stress, such as cortisol patterns. Cortisol is a stress hormone with natural daily highs and lows. Acute and chronic stress flatten the slopes of daily cortisol patterns. Positive conflict behaviors predict healthier daily cortisol patterns, while scorn (a specific negative behavior) was associated with flatter slope patterns (Bierstetel & Slatcher, 2020). The findings associated with cortisol and cardiovascular functioning highlight the reciprocal nature of romantic partner conflict and stress-related physical functioning.

Reconciliation is a critical conflict behavior for maintaining satisfying and functional romantic relationships. A thorough reconciliation process can be defined as one in which one party makes amends and the other party grants forgiveness (Schrage et al., 2020). In relationships, reconciliation is any behavior made to repair the damage. To extend the definition of reconciliation, Gottman and Silver (1999) defined a repair as any statement or action which prevents negativity from escalating. As conflict is an inherent part of any relationship, the ability to make repairs is a necessary skill in every relationship. Perhaps the most fundamental repair skill is the ability to make a sincere apology. An effective apology conveys genuine remorse and empathy for the suffering of the victim and increases the victim's sense of peace with the offender as well as their willingness to interact with the offender in the future (Borinca et al., 2021). When people exist in a romantic relationship it is inevitable that the individuals will harm the other, intentionally, or unintentionally. The presence of such a conflict requires repair to avoid intensifying negativity. Repairs are a specific type of positive conflict behavior which help prevent the development of anger and resentment in a relationship.

Positive Behaviors. Positive conflict behaviors in a romantic relationship include any behavior during a conflict situation that improves the outcome and perception of the conflict. In a study examining the role of conflict behavior on cortisol patterns, the three behaviors coded as 'positive' were affection, humor, and engagement (Bierstetel & Slatcher, 2020). Engagement in this sense is different than other uses of 'conflict engagement' which more closely align with conflict escalation. As a positive behavior, engagement refers to a partner's ability to be present and contribute to the discussion, a synonym for participation. In another study exploring the role of oxytocin in couples' communications, the positive behaviors were coded as affectionate or validating (Roels et al., 2021). Conflict management and resolution styles are characterized by behaviors. Constructive strategies are those marked by an openness to a conversation (engagement), accepting the partner's point of view (validating), and a commitment to solving the problem (Delatorre & Wagner, 2019). Behaviors categorized as positive create a sense of 'we'-ness wherein the partners stand together against a problem rather than partners pitted against each other.

Negative Behaviors. In contrast, negative conflict behaviors are those which harm the intimacy and connection of partners. Two broad categories of destructive strategies are those characterized by attacking or avoiding behaviors (Delatorre & Wagner, 2019). While a host of behaviors fall under each type, negative behaviors are typically categorized in one of these two ways. Specific types of negative conflict behavior include disengagement, defensiveness, aggressiveness, scorn, and frustration (Bierstetel & Slatcher, 2020). The study also coded anxiety and hurt as negative conflict behaviors, but they were omitted as they are emotional reactions and not specific types of behavior. Other negative conflict behaviors include hostility and controlling behaviors (Smith et al., 2021), retaliation, possessiveness, and violence (Dardis & Gidycz, 2019). These negative behaviors not only reduce the likelihood that the specific conflict will resolve satisfactorily but also decrease the overall health and satisfaction of the relationship.

Uncategorized Behaviors. Because real life is not black and white, there are some types of behaviors that do not fit neatly into 'positive' or 'negative.' These labels exist as a result of the consequences of the behavior (beneficial or harmful) rather than the inherent properties of the behavior. Some types of behavior can be either beneficial or harmful depending on the context, relationship, motivation, and other factors. In the Romantic Partner Conflict Scale, three of the behaviors which do not fit into either positive or negative classification are avoidance, submission, and separation (Zacchilli et al., 2009). Avoidance is the practice of preventing a conflict situation from starting and is generally categorized as a negative conflict behavior; however, there is wisdom in recognizing an appropriate time to engage in a conflict interaction with a partner. Separation is the practice of creating physical distance (e.g., walking away, going for a drive) in the middle of a conflict. Again, this is typically considered a negative behavior, unless it is used by partners to physically de-escalate (Gottman & Levenson, 1992). An important factor here is that conflict is not left to fester and that the behaviors are used to foster more productive conflict interactions.

Invariably humans seek out romantic relationships because relationships fulfill physical, psychological, and social needs. Romantic partnerships are heavily influenced by time and culture (Hoplock & Stinson, 2021). Types of romantic partner variations include marital, cohabitating non-marital, homosexual, heterosexual, monogamous, and polyamorous. Despite cultural variations in the structure of the relationship, satisfying romantic relationships improve overall well-being (Kansky, 2018). The importance of romantic relationships for personal well-being led to a variety of research on the characteristics of healthy versus unhealthy relationships. Primary predictors of relationship quality include partner responsiveness, emotion regulation, and conflict interactions (Slatcher & Schoebi, 2017). As conflict is a primary predictor of relationship health, factors associated with positive conflict skills and strategies merit further discussion (cite with current citation). Associated with personal and interpersonal benefits, mindfulness is implicated in academic literature to improve conflict situations.

Mindfulness

The word mindfulness is a translation of an ancient Buddhist term and has traveled across time and space to become a pervasive theme in psychology research and mental health treatment. In traditional Buddhist practices, mindfulness is one part of a three-part practice for self-transformation through calming the mind, reducing self-centeredness, and cultivating mental resilience (Pemaratana & Khong, 2021). With its introduction to Western cultures, mindfulness has become synonymous with a variety of cognitive processes, most commonly sustained attention (Dawson, 2021). Psychological research around mindfulness increased dramatically in recent years. Mindfulness now has a place in several evidence-based treatment interventions including dialectical behavior therapy, mindfulness-based cognitive therapy, acceptance and commitment therapy, and mindfulness-based stress reduction (Baer et al., 2006). From traditional to contemporary, the core mindfulness conceptualizations and practices are unchanged.

Traditional. The subcontinent of India includes a rich history of mindfulness practices including yoga, meditation, and chanting. Northeast India is the birthplace of Buddhism which features mindfulness as a core principle, and Buddhism, along with mindfulness, spread to other parts of Asia over 2500 years ago (Garcia-Campayo et al., 2021). The original Buddhist texts were written in Sanskrit, an ancient Indian language, and have been translated, resulting in the development of terms including mindfulness. In the texts, the word translated as mindfulness is often *smrti* which is also translated as 'bare attention' and even 'memory' (Garcia-Campayo et al., 2021). Smrti as a concept was formalized into a set of practices under the umbrella term mindfulness meditation. Three types of mindfulness include a focus on the breath, attention to the impermanence of physical sensations, and directing goodwill to self and others (Kakumanu et al., 2018). These are the three most basic forms of practicing traditional mindfulness. As time passed and Buddhism spread geographically, the beliefs and practices became increasingly diverse.

Mindfulness is predominant in both ancient and contemporary practices of Chinese Zen Buddhism. The goal of Zen practices is to awaken the nature of self as empty and to recognize the illusion of separateness (Ramm, 2021). The nature of the self as empty or void refers to the belief that there is no individual self with skin and personality, but rather an inner energy that is the same across all living beings. The illusion of separation refers to the belief that the perception of distinct 'selves' is erroneous. Again, within the Zen context, mindfulness is only one part of a larger practice. Zen Buddhist practices include concentration, insight, higher attainment, trance, wisdom, stream-entry, seeing one's nature, understanding, and the realm of illusion in addition to mindfulness (Jiang et al., 2018). Mindfulness in the Zen tradition serves a specific purpose. Mindful concentration is used to integrate the mind and body to achieve a state where the consciousness is solely in the body, called 'no mind' (Sakuta, 2018). Mindfulness in Zen Buddhism and traditional Buddhism serve the purpose of increasing concentration and uniting mind and body.

While Zen Buddhism is common in China, Theravada Buddhism is strongest in Southeast Asia. According to Theravada Buddhism, it is important to practice mindfulness in conjunction with the other two pillars of Buddha's teachings, which are generosity and morality (Pemaratana & Khong, 2021). Mindfulness, generosity, and morality are implicated as three equally important practices in this tradition of Buddhism. Scholars of Theravada Buddhism refer to the Dhammas, the three pillars of Buddhism, as a practical method for regulating the mind and emotions (Skilton et al., 2019). The pragmatism of the Buddhist method for applying the Dhammas lies in the discrete instructions provided for engaging in meditation and mindfulness practices combined with ever-present generosity and morality. There is a great variety in traditional mindfulness meditation practices in terms of content and technique (Skilton et al., 2019). The emphasis on generosity and morality is exemplified in the popular 'loving-kindness' meditation. The loving kindness meditation or Metta meditation begins with kind affirmations toward the self and expanded to include all others (Pemaratana & Khong, 2021). The traditional Buddhist mindfulness roots are inextricably linked with generosity and morality.

There is much debate in the academic and spiritual communities over the use of mindfulness in contemporary psychological and clinical settings. Some argue that secular (nonspiritual) practices of mindfulness increase narcissism and egocentrism, which is in direct opposition to the traditional roots of mindfulness, wherein the purpose is to enable the individual to live more intimately and freely with the world (Dawson, 2021). If one believes that the root of suffering is found in a sense of separateness from the world, then a mindfulness practice which increases egotism would increase rather than decrease suffering. Others propose that discrepancies between traditional Buddhist and contemporary research or clinical definitions are not only inevitable but also not inherently problematic (Baer, 2019). This same research identifies inconsistencies in traditional Buddhist definitions of mindfulness as partially responsible for the differences between Buddhist and psychological conceptions, while also pointing out that mainstream mindfulness is a separate entity and does contain some misconceptions. Secularizing mindfulness for research and treatment alters the traditional concept while making the practice more widely accessible. Academic debate continues over the consequences of altering mindfulness as a spiritual practice, and many contemporary researchers and teachers have attempted to maintain the traditional roots.

Contemporary. Contemporary mindfulness refers to theories, studies, and practices conducted by Western academics and clinicians. Mainstream (pop culture) mindfulness is distinct from contemporary psychological concepts and contains some important misconceptions (Baer, 2019). Contemporary leaders in the field of mindfulness include Jon Kabat-Zinn and Thich Nhat Hanh who are credited with popularizing mindfulness in the West, and Marsha Linehan who included mindfulness as one of four primary areas of skill development in her revolutionary treatment approach. Mindfulness has experienced a relatively recent and objectively dramatic surge in academic presence expanding from one published article in 1982 to 692 published articles by 2017 (Baer, 2019). In general, the literature supports the effectiveness of mindfulness interventions for improving a host of physical, psychological, and social symptoms; however, some studies documented the negative effects of mindfulness. The following is a discussion of the theories, treatment interventions, observed benefits, and rationale for the perceived negative effects of mindfulness.

There is ample peer-reviewed, academically sound, interdisciplinary research on the benefits of mindfulness for physical health. The most direct link between mindfulness and physical health is stress appraisals, with those lower in mindfulness experiencing more negative stress appraisals and worse health outcomes (O'Loughlin et al., 2019). Stress appraisals is a term used to describe the different ways that people mentally evaluate life situations. Research supports mindfulness interventions as an effective way to reduce stress and improve pain management in people with various chronic illnesses (Alsubaie et al., 2017). In addition to ameliorating the negative somatic effects of stress, mindfulness directly improves the experience of physical symptoms. A meta-analysis of 29 randomized controlled trials resulted in the documentation of statistically significant improvement in pain, fatigue, and sleep disturbances for cancer patients and survivors after mindfulness-based interventions (Cillessen et al., 2019). Mindfulness-based interventions not only decreased the negative effects of stress on physical health but also improved pain management, sleep quality, and fatigue.

One of the first mindfulness-based intervention programs was Jon Kabat-Zinn's program through the University of Massachusetts Medical Center. Established in 1979, the official mindfulness-based stress reduction (MBSR) clinic consists of eight weekly group sessions and one full-day retreat with formal mindfulness meditation and yoga practices, as well as informal activities to be practiced daily and during stressful situations (Hazlett-Stevens, 2018). Over the 40 years since its inception, MBSR has provided a platform for studying the effects of mindfulness practices in a variety of settings. Recent literature includes evidence of benefits for healthcare professionals (Lamothe et al., 2020), those suffering from lower quality of life from tinnitus (Chatterjee et al., 2021), and pregnant women (Skovbjerg et al., 2021). The MBSR highlights several key themes, including the pervasive negative physical, psychological, and social consequences of stress, and the usefulness of mindfulness in relieving those negative effects.

The psychological benefits of mindfulness include both cognitive and emotional dimensions. Mindfulness is a buffer between anxiety, suicidal ideation, and attempts (Brooks et al., 2021). Typically, elevated sensitivity to anxiety is associated with increased suicidal ideation and the risk of a suicide attempt; however, the buffering effect of mindfulness negates this relationship so that increased anxiety sensitivity does not correlate with increased suicidality. One rationale for the strong association between mindfulness and positive mental health outcomes is the practice of non-attachment, non-reactivity, and letting go of the need for control (Karing et al., 2021). These dimensions exist in addition to merely directing and sustaining attention. In a study on mindfulness as a mediating factor for adverse childhood experiences (ACE) and adult symptomology, the nonjudging of inner experiences facet of mindfulness successfully disrupted the relationship between ACE and generalized anxiety (Dolbier et al., 2021). Taken together, this research supports the effectiveness of mindfulness as a protective and corrective force for mental health.

In addition to MBSR, several popular psychotherapy treatments feature mindfulness as a prominent intervention. Psychotherapies featuring mindfulness (among other distinguishing concepts) are referred to as 'third wave' therapies in contrast to first-wave behaviorism and second-wave cognitive behaviorism (Rosales & Tan, 2017). Acceptance and Commitment Therapy (ACT) is an accepted, evidence-based treatment featuring mindfulness as an underlying concept of four (acceptance, defusion, contact with present, and self as context) out of six (values and committed action remain) core processes (Casey et al., 2020). As the name suggests, the increased psychological flexibility through the application of the six core processes empowers the individual to engage more effectively with internal (acceptance) and external (commitment) aspects of their existence. In Mindfulness-Based Cognitive Therapy (MBCT) the goal is to change the relationship of the patient with their negative thought patterns by decentering from the thought (Rosales & Tan, 2017). Decentering from the thought is the process of dis-identifying by recognizing that one is experiencing a thought rather than being defined by that thought (i.e., my thoughts happen to me versus I am my thoughts). Both ACT and MBCT feature aspects of mindfulness but are less popular in psychotherapy than Dialectical Behavior Therapy.

Developed by Marsha Linehan, Dialectical Behavior Therapy is an evidence-based treatment featuring mindfulness as a primary intervention. The DBT was developed to specifically meet the needs of people diagnosed with borderline personality disorder (BPD), but a growing body of research supports its effectiveness with other disorders including depression and anxiety (Mochrie et al., 2019). The overlap in the symptoms of BPD with other disorders may explain, at least in part, the effectiveness of DBT for a range of psychopathologies. The Borderline Personality Disorder is characterized by unstable moods, relationships, behaviors, thought processes, behaviors, and self-image (Mitchell et al., 2019). The effectiveness of DBT skills and treatment for a variety of mental health disorders suggests an element of generalizability in the treatment model. The DBT has the stated goal of helping clients toward a life worth living and starts by working to eliminate life-threatening behaviors (Warlick et al., 2020). The variety of evidence-based treatments featuring mindfulness supports its standing as a valid construct in psychological science.

In addition to the individual benefits, mindfulness is associated with prosocial behaviors. An analysis of five studies supported the effectiveness of mindfulness interventions to increase prosocial behavior (helping, guidance, compassionate responding, and financial assistance) in work-related environments (Hafenbrack et al., 2020). Prosocial behaviors are often viewed as an essential element of any functional social environment. Mindfulness intervention also produced improved prosocial behaviors in kindergartners as measured by kindness, helpfulness, consideration, and sharing as well as decreased impulsivity and hyperactivity (Viglas & Perlman, 2018). These two analyses were selected to highlight the demonstrated benefits of mindfulness interventions across the lifespan and in different settings. Prosocial behavior includes any behavior intended to benefit another person and includes affective and cognitive processes, many of which are associated with mindfulness (Donald et al., 2019). As an important foundation for societal functioning, prosocial behaviors have been the target of both academic research and religious teachings.

Thich Nhat Hanh is a Buddhist monk who worked to make mindfulness accessible to Western cultures. A Vietnamese Buddhist monk and peace activist, Hanh co-founded Plum Village, a retreat center in France (Hagens, 2017). Plum Village is a place where Buddhist monks live, and anyone can visit and engage with the monks to learn and practice mindfulness. Engaging non-violently with the world, Hanh developed the community of interbeing which exists as a network of connected, unified people and incorporates a blend of traditional mindfulness practices (Scherer & Waistell, 2018). The term interbeing refers to the use of mindfulness for connecting with oneself, the world, and each other. Hanh coined the term interbeing and describes its associated principles as a way to explain Buddha's teachings in a way that lay people can understand (Lim, 2019). Bringing Buddhism from Vietnam to France, and explaining Buddha's teachings in an accessible way, Hanh is a primary figure in establishing a traditional thread of mindfulness in contemporary culture.

While there is ample evidence to support the benefits of mindfulness interventions, it is important to acknowledge the presence of evidence suggesting negative outcomes. A small number of studies noted agitation, suicidal ideation, and depression as a result of mindfulness meditation (Lutkajtis, 2019). The presence of adverse effects of mindfulness meditation is important to acknowledge, but perhaps even more important to understand. One study even suggested that adverse effects may be a normal part of meditation practice (Lutkajtis, 2018). One possible explanation is that the expectation that mindfulness, also sometimes translated as 'bare attention,' only result in pleasurable experiences is unrealistic. In traditional Buddhist practices, unwanted effects are considered natural and inherent to the process (Cebolla et al., 2017). If taught as a purely attentive process, it is reasonable that some individuals may have adverse reactions to paying attention to thoughts, sensations, and emotions. Normally, attention will fall on both comfortable and uncomfortable things. Dispositional mindfulness is a description of mindfulness which includes not only attentive processes but also those associated with compassion and acceptance featured in the more common conceptualization.

Trait or Dispositional. To study a concept, it must be broken into core elements which can be measured. Growing out of the model and definition of mindfulness provided by Jon Kabat-Zinn, dispositional mindfulness is the philosophy that mindfulness can be separated into distinct cognitive and behavioral activities. While some people may naturally possess some or all of the skills, an important aspect of any skill is that it can be taught and learned (Baer, 2019). In this way, mindfulness is not an enigmatic or spiritual practice which makes it inaccessible to the general population. Despite the exclusion of a spiritual component, the discussion of mindfulness as a set of practicable skill aligns with its traditional Buddhist roots. The five-facet structure of mindfulness proposes that mindfulness can be broken down into observing, describing, non-judgment, acting with awareness, and non-reactivity to internal events (Karl & Fischer, 2020). The validity and reliability of the five-facet mindfulness questionnaire is discussed in the validity and reliability sections. What follows is a discussion of the conceptual background of each of the identified facets of mindfulness.

Dispositional mindfulness operationalizes the concept as levels of observing, describing, non-judging, acting with awareness, and non-reactivity to inner experience. Observing is the act of noticing internal and external sensations which includes thoughts and emotions (Meng et al., 2020). This trait is the most directly linked to the common misconception that mindfulness is merely the act of paying attention alone. Some hypothesize that this misconception could be harmful, and that true mindfulness has a quality of warmth, compassion, and interest (Baer, 2019). Observing alone is not an adequate definition of mindfulness. The second dimension of mindfulness is describing. Describing is the ability and predisposition to use words to recount internal and external observations (Karl & Fischer, 2020). Describing, therefore, includes processes involving language and communication. This could include interpersonal activities (conversation) or individual processes (journaling). The first two dimensions of mindfulness, observing and describing, incorporate the cognitive processes needed for attention and language.

Acting with awareness is another mindfulness disposition associated with attention. Acting with awareness encompasses two separate attentive processes. The first is being attentive to an activity (Meng et al., 2020). The second is sustaining undivided focus (Karl & Fischer, 2020). Sustaining undivided focus is the practice of or ability to resist distractions, which is a separate cognitive task from being aware of a task. Acting with awareness is often discussed in opposition to the tendency for humans to behave on autopilot. Autopilot is the tendency for humans to engage in a physical task while their attention is elsewhere (Gu et al., 2016). Acting with awareness is a mindful disposition combining two cognitive tasks related to attention: focusing on one thing and resisting distraction by others.

Non-judging and non-reactivity to inner experience are facets of mindfulness indirectly associated with attention. Nonjudging of inner experience is the practice of accepting thoughts and emotions without evaluating them (Karl & Fischer, 2020). This means not labeling them as either good or bad, right, or wrong, or even helpful or unhelpful. The non-judging element incorporates themes found in traditional Buddhist mindfulness such as compassion, acceptance, and friendliness. Non-reactivity to inner experience includes both recognizing inner experiences as temporary (Karl & Fischer, 2020), and noticing thoughts, feelings, and emotions without reacting to them (Meng et al., 2020). Non-reactivity to inner experience is the facet of mindfulness from the five-facet mindfulness paradigm most directly linked to emotion regulation.

Over the last 2500 years, mindfulness has emerged as a practice to benefit individuals and society. Born in India as part of the Theravada Buddhist tradition, mindfulness was practiced in conjunction with generosity and morality (Pemaratana & Khong, 2021). Traveling to Western cultures, mindfulness was changed in a variety of ways. Some maintained the traditional roots of the practices while excluding religious affiliation to make the practice more widely available (Baer, 2019). Others attempted to teach mindfulness without training or education in the multi-faceted practice of mindfulness leading to criticisms of cultivating narcissism and egotism (Dawson, 2021). The five-facet mindfulness structure both maintains the traditional roots of mindfulness and operationalizes the concept for psychological study and use in therapeutic interventions. The five-facet mindfulness paradigm also highlights overlapping content areas with current literature on romantic relationships.

Points of Convergence

Theoretically, mindfulness is typically discussed as it relates only to the individual, but there are several places where mindfulness and romantic relationships overlap. Several keywords appear throughout research on romantic relationship and on mindfulness. These keywords include stress, emotion regulation, attention, attachment, kindness, non-judgment, acceptance, and the ability to be present (being). The presence of the same themes throughout research on both concepts suggests similar mechanisms by which each function. These overlapping content areas, or points of convergence, substantiate the validity of research which explores a correlation between the two seemingly unrelated constructs.

Stress. Stress is a central focus in both mindfulness and romantic partner research. Jarvela-Reijonen et al. (2020) pointed out there is no uniform definition for stress, but responses to stressful situations involve psychological and physiological processes. Therefore, stress is an internal (mental and physical) response to some event which could be a thought, feeling, or external situation. Stress appraisals exist in two stages; 1) evaluation of the situation followed by 2) evaluation of the resources available to manage it (O'Loughlin et al., 2019). Stressors exist as either chronic (e.g., financial worries) or acute (e.g., an active conflict situation) and both types are present in romantic relationships. Coping effectively with stress allows individuals to alleviate the negative feeling and regulate reactions to the stressful event (stressor; Tekel & Erus, 2020). Mindfulness is an effective way to manage both chronic and acute stressors (Jarvela-Reijonen et al., 2020; Karremans et al., 2020; Lamothe et al., 2020; Tekel & Erus, 2020). Stress is a notable area of overlapping academic research for two primary reasons. First, stress has a direct negative impact on relationship functioning. Second, literature supports mindfulness as an effective stress management strategy.

Emotion Regulation. Because there is a propensity for intense emotion and the physical stress response during conflict, emotion regulation is highlighted as a necessary skill for effective conflict management and resolution. Gottman and Levenson (1992) is an example of the successful use of emotion regulation during conflict to predict marital satisfaction and dissolution, which suggests that emotion regulation during conflict situations strongly influences relationship health. Mindfulness is also directly related to emotion regulation. Describing, acting with awareness, non-reactivity, and non-judging are all facets of mindfulness, which are strongly associated with the ability to identify, modulate, and respond effectively to emotions (MacDonald, 2021). Unsurprisingly, during conflict situations one or both partners experience difficult emotions, so the ability to identify and manage the emotion is necessary to resolve the conflict and avoid escalating negativity. The goal is not to suppress emotions during conflict, as Thomson et al., (2018) provided evidence that emotion suppression during conflict actually reduced the chances of effective resolution. Emotion regulation allows for appropriate communication and response to difficult emotions which arise naturally during conflict situations.

Being versus Doing. Mindfulness may facilitate more positive conflict interactions between partners through activation of the being mode rather than the doing mode. The doing mode refers to analytical problem-solving which can devolve into self-focused problem-solving, leading to beliefs that the problem is within the self or even unsolvable (Rosales & Tan, 2017). The doing mode, while prioritizing action to mitigate a perceived problem also perpetuates separateness between individuals. The being mode, or embodiment, is an enlightened state wherein one transcends the mind barrier of separation between self and others (Sakuta, 2018). Transitioning to a state of being allows an individual to recognize their interconnectedness with others. The being mode is a sense of openness and non-judgment which allows for full engagement with the present moment, thereby increasing responsiveness and decreasing rumination about past pain or future anxieties (Rosales & Tan, 2017). Conflict situations happen in the present moment, so the ability to respond in the present moment without the influence of past memories, future worries, or extreme emotions may be one mechanism by which mindfulness affects romantic partner conflict behaviors.

Attachment. Buddhist and Western psychology both feature attachment as a core concept underlying one's ability to connect. Western psychology conceptualizes attachment as the ability (or inability) to make bonds with others through internalization of the responsiveness and accessibility of a caregiver and then other relationships such as romantic partners (Paquette et al., 2020). Using this definition, stable connections with others rely on early childhood experiences and another person's ability to consistently help the other feel both safe and free simultaneously. Seemingly contradictory, Buddhist psychology features a strong emphasis on non-attachment, defined as a release from mental fixations (Sahdra & Shaver, 2013). Though on the surface it seems that Western culture advocates attachment while Buddhist psychology rejects it, this is not accurate. Buddhist psychology associates attachment with grasping or clinging to a mental distortion (Sahdra et al., 2010) but it does support having connections with others that are based on love (Ghose, 2004). The shift from attachment as clinging to attachment as a connection has important theoretical and clinical applications. Implicating mindfulness as a mechanism in this process, increased levels of mindfulness are associated with decreased negative effects of attachment insecurity on couples' conflict behaviors (Quickert & MacDonald, 2020). Both Buddhist and Western psychology emphasize the need for supportive connections, and mindfulness may be a way to facilitate this in adults despite the development of insecure attachment patterns in childhood.

Attention. In Western cultures, mindfulness is almost always associated with attention. Recent empirical literature supported the effectiveness of mindfulness to improve executive attention (Lin et al., 2019), and trait mindfulness included observing as one of the five central facets of mindfulness (Baer et al., 2006). Attention in this context refers to directing and sustaining full awareness on the events of the present moment. This type of attention may decrease the intense negative emotions felt during a conflict by removing attention from personal concerns thereby reducing discomfort and increasing task accuracy (in this case, conflict resolution; Petranker & Eastwood, 2021). Partner responsiveness refers to a partner's ability to respond in the moment to the needs of their partner and is associated with higher levels of relationship well-being. Partners higher in mindfulness were perceived as having higher responsiveness during discussions of partner vulnerability (Khalifian & Barry, 2021). Increased responsiveness and decreased negative affect are two ways attention could be a mechanism for an association between mindfulness and romantic partner conflict behaviors.

Non-Judgmental Acceptance. Nonjudgmental acceptance is a term almost exclusively used in mindfulness research referred to in other psychology research as psychological flexibility. In mindfulness research, non-judging or non-judgmental acceptance is typically referring to an internal experience such as a thought or emotion (Baer et al., 2006; Karl & Fischer, 2020). Logically, this process is associated with improved emotion regulation and has also been applied to romantic relationship functioning. Non-judgmental acceptance can also be the ability to acknowledge a partner's shortcomings or annoyances without feeling the urge to change them (Karremans et al., 2017). This requires the partner to be willing to adjust their ideals of a partner or their relationship. Psychological flexibility is characterized by an accepting element which allows individuals to shift their mindset, adapt to situational demands, and adjust behaviors to accommodate social and personal functioning (Twiselton et al., 2020). The ability to accept a person, situation, thought, or feeling without evaluation is a skill which empowers the individual to choose from a host of prosocial behaviors.

Loving-Kindness. In traditional mindfulness practices, loving-kindness is a meditation that directs well wishes and compassion first to oneself and then to an identified other (Pemaratana & Khong, 2021). While not using the exact same terminology, affection surfaces frequently in empirical literature on romantic relationships. Affection is often identified and coded as an example of positive behavior during a conflict situation (see Bierstetel & Slatcher, 2020; Roels et al., 2021). Kindness is not only beneficial when expressed between partners, but also when cultivated individually. Self-compassion is associated both with positive problem-solving and decreased compliance during conflict situations (Tandler et al., 2021). These findings are notable because they imply that mindfulness is a prosocial force beyond emotion regulation and attention. This supports the need to include traditional Buddhist mindfulness principles (such as compassion and friendliness) into contemporary mindfulness interventions.

On the surface, mindfulness and romantic partner research may appear to have little in common. However, after a thorough discussion of current empirical literature several common themes emerged. Themes in romantic partner research included the importance of partner responsiveness, affection, emotion regulation, and positive conflict strategies. Themes of mindfulness research are compassionate acceptance of all experiences and awareness of the present moment. The identified points of convergence are stress, emotion regulation, non-judgmental acceptance, attention, attachment, loving-kindness, and the states of being versus doing. The numerous points of convergence in the literature support continued empirical exploration of a predictive relationship between mindfulness and romantic partner conflict strategies.

Problem Statement

It was not known if and to what extent the five mechanisms of mindfulness identified in the Five Facet Mindfulness Questionnaire predict the six conflict strategy subdomains identified in the Romantic Partner Conflict Scale used by adults in a committed romantic relationship. Theoretical literature exists which hypothesizes the processes by which mindfulness could improve romantic conflict interactions (Karremans et al., 2017); however, it is necessary to have empirical evidence to support theoretical modeling. There is empirical evidence to support some facets of mindfulness as statistically significant predictors of some conflict strategies; however, the two exploratory studies both cite insufficient evidence due to limitations in the featured mindfulness measure (see Harvey et al., 2015; Harvey et al., 2019). Current academic literature acknowledges that seemingly contradictory evidenced related to mindfulness is likely caused by incomplete operationalization (Baer, 2019); therefore, it is essential to include all identified facets of mindfulness before concluding whether or not mindfulness is a significant predictor of romantic relationship conflict strategies. Despite empirical and theoretical literature, there was insufficient evidence to conclude which mechanisms of mindfulness predict conflict strategy use between adults in a committed romantic relationship.

The population of interest was adults in the Mid-Atlantic region of the United States who are in committed romantic relationships. A population of interest includes all those to whom the results could potentially be generalized (Lavrakas, 2008). However, the generalizability of a study depends on a number of significant factors, so the study may not generalize appropriately to the entire population of interest. Conflict is inevitable in committed romantic relationships and the study is therefore applicable to every person in a committed romantic relationship within the geographic area of interest.

Romantic partner conflict is inevitable but can be either beneficial or harmful to the functioning and well-being of individuals and relationships. Negative conflict behaviors are associated with lower levels of overall relationship satisfaction (Zacchilli et al., 2009) while positive conflict behaviors are associated with greater feelings of support and intimacy (Becker et al., 2017). Some behaviors cannot be categorized as inherently negative or positive because the consequences depend heavily on the context within which they are exhibited. The first step in developing an evidence-based intervention to improve relationships via improved conflict is to establish if and to what extent specific mechanisms of mindfulness predict conflict strategy use. Improved conflict is defined as increase presence of constructive conflict strategies alongside decreased presence of harmful conflict strategies. After establishing predictive power, a variety of experimental studies should examine the effectiveness of an intervention in achieving the desired outcome. This study serves to support or reject a recommendation for future research to determine if mindfulness training is an effective intervention for improving conflict interactions in adult romantic relationships. These recommendations are discussed in detail in Chapter 5.

Summary

The purpose of Chapter 2 is to lay out a clear and concise review of relevant theories and literature for the purpose of demonstrating a need for the proposed research study including all methodological choices. Albert Chavannes, the founder of social exchange theory, posits that the foundation of a successful society rests in the perception of beneficial interactions between members (Chavannes, 1898). Most cultures include the expectation that individuals will maintain a romantic relationship. Furthermore, romantic relationships include innumerable exchanges between the same members and have a strong influence on members' mental and physical health. Conflict is a type of social exchange that occurs in every relationship and has the potential to benefit or harm the relationship and its members. Couples' behaviors during conflict can be used to accurately predict the maintenance or dissolution of the relationship (Kim et al., 2007). Current literature already implicated mindfulness as a significant influence on couples' conflict exchanges; however, there is insufficient evidence to document which mechanisms of mindfulness predict conflict strategy use between partners.

Mindfulness recently emerged at the forefront of psychological research and already includes theoretical and empirical ties to personal and social functioning. Jon Kabat-Zinn developed the Mindfulness-Based Stress Reduction program using a combination of mindfulness meditation principles to reduce symptoms of stress related to a variety of physical and mental health conditions (Hazlett-Stevens, 2018). The MBSR program and the work of Jon Kabat-Zinn represent the transformation of mindfulness from a fringe spiritual concept to contemporary clinical and academic use. Kabat-Zinn (2003) defines mindfulness as the practice of bringing one's attention to some aspect of the present moment in a non-judgmental way. This definition is most accurately captured by the five-facet mindfulness questionnaire which established observing, describing, non-judging, acting with awareness, and non-reactivity as the five components of mindfulness (Baer et al., 2006). There are numerous points of convergence in romantic partner conflict and mindfulness research including themes such as stress, emotion regulation, attachment, and kindness. The documented effectiveness of mindfulness in increasing prosocial behaviors combined with the demonstrated need to identify ways to improve romantic partner conflict interactions supports the empirical exploration of a predictive association between romantic partner conflict and mindfulness.

Chapter 3: Methodology

Introduction

It was not known if and to what extent the five mechanisms of mindfulness identified in the Five Facet Mindfulness Questionnaire predict the six conflict strategy subdomains identified in the Romantic Partner Conflict Scale used by adults in a committed romantic relationship. Society is made of people and most people will exist in a romantic relationship at some point in their life. The health and functioning of that relationship have a significant impact on the well-being of the individual (Braithwaite & Holt-Lunstad, 2017); therefore, to improve the overall functioning of society, it is important to understand and develop ways of improving romantic relationships. Conflict is heavily implicated in the literature as a key element in the health of a relationship (Delatorre & Wagner, 2019; Kim et al., 2007) and there are several points of convergence between romantic partner and mindfulness research which implicate mindfulness and romantic partner conflict to have a predictive association.

The process of establishing a quantifiable predictive association requires specific data collection and data analysis procedures. This chapter enumerates all of the processes for transforming background data and a research topic into research questions, participant recruitment, data collection, and data analysis. There is also discussion of why a quantifiable predictive association is the most appropriate choice given the current empirical literature on the subject. Instrumentation, validity, reliability, limitations, and delimitations are also explored and rationalized. This section ends by highlighting the ethical considerations for the study.

Purpose of the Study

The purpose of this quantitative predictive correlational study was to determine if and to what extent the five mechanisms of mindfulness identified in the Five Facet Mindfulness Questionnaire predict the six conflict strategy subdomains identified in the Romantic Partner Conflict Scale used by adults in a committed romantic relationship living in the mid-Atlantic region of the United States. The study consists of the five predictor variables (the facets of mindfulness in the FFMQ) and six criterion variables (romantic partner conflict subdomains in the RPCS). Data on these variables was gathered using the five-facet mindfulness questionnaire – 15-item short version (FFMQ - 15) and the romantic partner conflict scale (RPCS). The proposal was that data would then be analyzed using descriptive statistics and linear regression. The linear regression would be used to answer research questions 1-5. RQ1-5 examines the extent to which each mindfulness trait predicts the conflict strategy subdomains during conflict interactions between romantic partners. Linear regression results in an R-squared value which is interpreted as the extent to which change in the predictor variable accounts for the change in the outcome (or criterion) variable. Therefore, the data analysis would yield information on the extent to which changes in facets of mindfulness (from the FFMQ-15) account for the change in the prevalence of the conflict strategy subdomains (from the RPCS). The instruments selected to measure the variables and to support the research questions are founded on Jon Kabat-Zinn's model of mindfulness and social exchange theory. Relevant changes are discussed in Chapters 4 and 5.

Research Questions and Hypotheses

The research questions and hypotheses address the identified problem statement that it was not known if and to what extent the five mechanisms of mindfulness identified in the Five Facet Mindfulness Questionnaire predict conflict strategy use between adults in a committed romantic relationship. The proposed statistical analysis will include a two-tailed hypothesis test to determine the predictive correlative significance which serves as the basis to accept or reject the null hypotheses.

Table 3.1

Variable Table - Predictors

Variable	Conceptual Definition	Operational Definition	Measurement Level	Instrument/Data Source
Acting with Awareness	Acting with awareness encompasses two separate attentive processes. The first is being attentive to an activity (Meng et al., 2020). The second is sustaining undivided focus (Karl & Fischer, 2020).	Participant's score on items 3R, 8R, 13R on the FFMQ-15 where R stands for a reverse scored item	Ordinal (treated as interval for the purpose of statistical analysis; see Boone & Boone, 2012) Likert scale measuring from: 1- never or very rarely true, 2 – rarely true, 3 – sometimes true, 4- often true, 5 – very often or always true	Five Facet Mindfulness Questionnaire, 15-item version (FFMQ-15) – Baer et al. (2008) 3 questions
Observing	The act of noticing internal and external sensations which includes thoughts and emotions (Meng et al., 2020).	Participant's score on items 1, 6, and 11 on the FFMQ-15	Ordinal (treated as interval for the purpose of statistical analysis; see Boone & Boone, 2012) 1-5 Likert scale	Five Facet Mindfulness Questionnaire, 15-item version (FFMQ-15) – Baer et al. (2008) 3 questions
Describing	The ability and predisposition to use words to recount internal and external observations (Karl & Fischer, 2020).	Participant's score on items 2, 7R, and 12 on the FFMQ-15	Ordinal (treated as interval for the purpose of statistical analysis; see Boone & Boone, 2012) 1-5 Likert scale	Five Facet Mindfulness Questionnaire, 15-item version (FFMQ-15) – Baer et al. (2008) 3 questions
Non-Reactivity	Recognizing inner experiences as temporary (Karl & Fischer, 2020) and noticing thoughts, feelings, and emotions without reacting to them (Meng et al., 2020).	Participant's score on items 5, 10, and 15 on the FFMQ-15	Ordinal (treated as interval for the purpose of statistical analysis; see Boone & Boone, 2012) 1-5 Likert scale	Five Facet Mindfulness Questionnaire, 15-item version (FFMQ-15) – Baer et al. (2008) 3 questions
Non-Judging	The practice of accepting thoughts and emotions without evaluating them (Karl & Fischer, 2020).	Participant's score on items 4R, 9R, and 14R on the FFMQ-15	Ordinal (treated as interval for the purpose of statistical analysis; see Boone & Boone, 2012) 1-5 Likert scale	Five Facet Mindfulness Questionnaire, 15-item version (FFMQ-15) – Baer et al. (2008) 3 questions

Table 3.2

Variable Table - Criterion

Variable	Conceptual Definition	Operational Definition	Measurement Level	Instrument/Data Source
Compromise	A strategy characterized by collaboration and negotiation; bounded by the goal of satisfying all partners' needs (Zacchilli et al., 2009)	Participant's score on items 1-14 of the RPCS	Ordinal (treated as interval for the purpose of statistical analysis; see Boone & Boone, 2012) 0-4 Likert scale	Romantic Partner Conflict Scale – Zacchilli et al. (2009) 39 questions
Avoidance	A strategy characterized by attempts to prevent a conflict before it occurs (Zacchilli et al., 2009)	Participant's score on items 15-17 of the RPCS	Ordinal (treated as interval for the purpose of statistical analysis; see Boone & Boone, 2012) 0-4 Likert scale	RPCS
Interactional Reactivity	A strategy characterized by aggression, volatility, and high expressed emotion (Zacchilli et al., 2009)	Participant's score on items 18-23 of the RPCS	Ordinal (treated as interval for the purpose of statistical analysis; see Boone & Boone, 2012) 0-4 Likert scale	RPCS
Separation	A strategy characterized by attempts to create physical distance to prevent escalation (Zacchilli et al., 2009)	Participant's score on items 24-28 of the RPCS	Ordinal (treated as interval for the purpose of statistical analysis; see Boone & Boone, 2012) 0-4 Likert scale	RPCS
Domination	A strategy characterized by attempts to win and be in control (Zacchilli et al., 2009)	Participant's score on items 29-34 of the RPCS	Ordinal (treated as interval for the purpose of statistical analysis; see Boone & Boone, 2012) 0-4 Likert scale	RPCS
Submission	A strategy characterized by giving in to the other and subjugating one's own needs for the other and/or to end the conflict (Zacchilli et al., 2009)	Participant's score on items 35-39 of the RPCS	Ordinal (treated as interval for the purpose of statistical analysis; see Boone & Boone, 2012) 0-4 Likert scale	RPCS

RQ1: Does acting with awareness predict conflict strategy subdomains used between adults in a committed romantic relationship?

H_o1: Acting with awareness does not predict conflict strategy use between adults in a committed romantic relationship for the following subdomains:

- Compromise
- Avoidance
- Interactional Reactivity
- Separation
- Domination
- Submission

H_a1: Acting with awareness predicts conflict strategy use between adults in a committed romantic relationship for the following subdomains:

- Compromise
- Avoidance
- Interactional Reactivity
- Separation
- Domination
- Submission

RQ2: Does observing predict conflict strategy subdomains used between adults in a committed romantic relationship?

H_o2: Observing does not predict conflict strategy use between adults in a committed romantic relationship for the following subdomains:

- Compromise
- Avoidance

- Interactional Reactivity
- Separation
- Domination
- Submission

H_a2: Observing predicts conflict strategy use between adults in a committed romantic relationship for the following subdomains:

- Compromise
- Avoidance
- Interactional Reactivity
- Separation
- Domination
- Submission

RQ3: Does describing predict conflict strategy subdomains used between adults in a committed romantic relationship?

H_o3: Describing does not predict conflict strategy use between adults in a committed romantic relationship for the following subdomains:

- Compromise
- Avoidance
- Interactional Reactivity
- Separation
- Domination
- Submission

H_a3: Describing predicts conflict strategy use between adults in a committed romantic relationship for the following subdomains:

- Compromise
- Avoidance
- Interactional Reactivity
- Separation
- Domination
- Submission

RQ4: Does non-judging predict conflict strategy subdomains used between adults in a committed romantic relationship?

H_o4: Non-judging does not predict conflict strategy use between adults in a committed romantic relationship for the following subdomains:

- Compromise
- Avoidance
- Interactional Reactivity
- Separation
- Domination
- Submission

H_a4: Non-judging predicts conflict strategy use between adults in a committed romantic relationship for the following subdomains:

- Compromise
- Avoidance
- Interactional Reactivity
- Separation
- Domination
- Submission

RQ5: Does non-reactivity predict conflict strategy subdomains used in conflict interactions between adults in a committed romantic relationship?

H_o5: Non-reactivity does not predict conflict strategy use between adults in a committed romantic relationship for the following subdomains:

- Compromise
- Avoidance
- Interactional Reactivity
- Separation
- Domination
- Submission

H_a5: Non-reactivity predicts conflict strategy use between adults in a committed romantic relationship for the following subdomains:

- Compromise
- Avoidance
- Interactional Reactivity
- Separation
- Domination
- Submission

Variables

The predictor and criterion variables included in the research questions are examined by type, conceptual and operational definitions, and data collection. Both instruments use ordinal Likert-scale data; however, the data will be treated as interval for the purposes of statistical analysis. Boone and Boone (2012) recommend using Likert-scale data as interval for use in Pearson's *r* parametric tests. This is a predictive study and will therefore use a T-test parametric test (provided all assumptions are met). All data is primary data collected via an online survey.

Acting with Awareness. The predictor variable for research question 1 and one of the five facets of mindfulness identified in the Five Facet Mindfulness Questionnaire. Conceptually, acting with awareness is describes as two separate attentive processes. The first is being attentive to an activity (Meng et al., 2020) and the second is sustaining undivided focus (Karl & Fischer, 2020). Operationally, acting with awareness is defined as the cumulative total of 3 items of the Five Facet Mindfulness Questionnaire – 15 item short form (FFMQ-15). Study participants will complete the FFMQ-15, which is composed of 5 subscales, and 15-items using a 5-point Likert scale. Acting with awareness is composed of items 3, 8, and 13 all of which must be reversed scored before being totaled for a cumulative subscale score.

Observing. The predictor variable for research question 2 and one of the five facets of mindfulness identified in the Five Facet Mindfulness Questionnaire. Observing is conceptually defined as the act of noticing internal and external sensations which includes thoughts and emotions (Meng et al., 2020). Operationally, observing is defined as a participant's score on items 1, 6, and 11 of the FFMQ-15. None of these items are reverse scored, so the participant totals on these items is summed for the subscale score.

Describing. The predictor variable for research question 3 and one of the five facets of mindfulness identified in the Five Facet Mindfulness Questionnaire. Describing is conceptually defined as the ability and predisposition to use words to recount internal and external observations (Karl & Fischer, 2020) and operationally defined as a participant's score on items 2, 7, and 12 of the FFMQ-15. Only item 7 is reverse scored on this subscale, so that item must be reversed before summing for a subscale total.

Non-Reactivity. The predictor variable for research question 4 and one of the five facets of mindfulness identified in the Five Facet Mindfulness Questionnaire. Non-reactivity is conceptually defined as recognizing inner experiences as temporary (Karl & Fischer, 2020) and noticing thoughts, feelings, and emotions without reacting to them (Meng et al., 2020). Operationally, non-reactivity is defined as a participant's score on items 5, 10, and 15 of the FFMQ-15. None of the items are reversed scored, so the subscale score is the summation of the item scores. The presence of the non-reactivity scale is a primary reason for selecting the FFMQ-15 for use in this study based on the cited importance of including non-reactivity as a dimension of mindfulness in Harvey et al. (2019).

Non-Judging. The predictor variable for research question 5 and one of the five facets of mindfulness identified in the Five Facet Mindfulness Questionnaire. Non-judging is conceptually defined as the practice of accepting thoughts and emotions without evaluating them (Karl & Fischer, 2020). Operationally, non-judging is defined as a participant's score on items 4, 9, and 14 of the FFMQ-15. All of the items are reversed scored, so the item scores must be reversed before being summed for the subscale score. The presence of the non-judging scale is a primary reason for selecting the FFMQ-15 for use in this study based on the cited importance of including non-judging as a dimension of mindfulness in Harvey et al. (2015).

Romantic Partner Conflict Strategies. There are six criterion variables for RQ1-5 which are the subdomains of romantic partner conflict strategies. These subdomains are compromise, avoidance, interactional reactivity, separation, domination, and submission. Chavannes (1898) defines conflict between partners as a state of disharmony which prohibits cooperation and problem solving. Conflict management and resolution strategies are the ways in which people attempt to manage or resolve this state of disharmony. Conflict strategies are operationalized in the Romantic Partner Conflict Scale (RPCS) as the presence of specific types of behavior during a conflict situation (Zacchilli et al., 2009). These behaviors fall into the categories of the conflict resolution and management strategies of compromise, interactional reactivity, domination, submission, avoidance, and separation. Study participants will complete the RPCS which includes 39-items divided into 6 subscales and using a 5-point Likert scale. There is one subscale for positive conflict behaviors (compromise), 2 subscales measuring negative conflict behaviors (interactional reactivity and domination), and 3 subscales which are uncategorized (submission, avoidance, and separation). Higher scores indicate greater presence of the conflict strategy whether positive, negative, or uncategorized.

Compromise. Conceptually defined as a strategy characterized by collaboration and negotiation while being bounded by the goal of satisfying all partners' needs (Zacchilli et al., 2009). Operationally defined as a participant's mean score on items 1-14 of the RPCS. This is the only conflict strategy subdomain from the RPCS which is exclusively correlated with positive relationship outcomes.

Avoidance. Conceptually defined as a strategy characterized by attempts to prevent a conflict before it occurs (Zacchilli et al., 2009). Operationally defined as a participant's mean score on items 15-17 of the RPCS. This conflict strategy subdomain is associated with relationship benefits and consequences which is attributed to the influence of important contextual factors (see Zacchilli et al., 2007).

Interactional Reactivity. Conceptually defined as a strategy characterized by aggression, volatility, and high expressed emotions (Zacchilli et al., 2009). Operationally defined as a participant's mean score on items 18-23 of the RPCS. This conflict strategy subdomain is associated exclusively with negative relationship outcomes.

Separation. Conceptually defined as a strategy characterized by attempts to create physical distance to prevent escalation during a conflict (Zacchilli et al., 2009). Operationally defined as a participant's mean score on items 24-28 of the RPCS. This conflict strategy subdomain is associated with relationship benefits and consequences which is attributed to the influence of important contextual factors (see Zacchilli et al., 2007).

Domination. Conceptually defined as a strategy characterized by attempts to win and be in control (Zacchilli et al., 2009). Operationally defined as a participant's mean score on items 29-34 of the RPCS. This conflict strategy subdomain is associated exclusively with negative relationship outcomes.

Submission. Conceptually defined as a strategy characterized by giving in to the other(s) and subjugating one's own needs to prioritize the other(s) and/or to end the conflict (Zacchilli et al., 2009). Operationally defined as a participant's mean score on items 35-39 of the RPCS. This conflict strategy subdomain is associated with relationship benefits and consequences which is attributed to the influence of important contextual factors (see Zacchilli et al., 2007).

Rationale for a Quantitative Methodology

The methodology selected for use in the research study is quantitative. This methodology uses interpretive statistics to analyze results from numerically collected data. Landrum and Garza (2015) highlights that quantitative studies are used to examine the relationship between two or more variables and that relationship is tested and verified through statistical analysis. The identification of variables and the statistical testing necessitate the creation of research hypotheses to be supported or refuted. The underlying assumption of quantitative research is that there is one single, identifiable 'truth' (Tuli, 2011, p. 100). The development and testing of hypotheses to uncover the 'truth' is unique and fundamental to the quantitative methodology. Quantitative methodology is most appropriate for studies with research questions which have definitive answers to hypotheses evidenced through statistics.

The research questions and hypotheses were written to align with the problem statement which was developed through identification of a problem space in current academic literature. In reference to a lack of statistical data available, Karremans et al. (2017) includes a need for future research to explore empirical evidence to support or refute conceptual frameworks implicating mindfulness as a benefit to romantic relationships. This implies that there is a single truth or quantifiable relationship to be examined between these two variables. In the research questions, the phrase '…does x predict y…' alongside the hypotheses 'X does or does not predict y…' aligns with the use of quantitative methodology to collect and analyze numerical data in order to support or refute a hypothesis. Other empirical studies include the use of quantitative methodology including Harvey et al. (2019) and Harvey et al. (2015) which yielded preliminary and insufficient support for mindfulness as a predictor of adult romantic partner conflict strategies. Given the identified variables, the literature supports the use of quantitative over qualitative or mixed methodology.

Qualitative and mixed methodologies would not be appropriate for the study. The purpose of a qualitative study is to capture an experiential or multidimensional event which transcends objective characterization (Jackson et al., 2007). Hypothesis testing, which is required to answer the identified research questions, is not a part of the qualitative methodology. After data collection, the data is coded and deducted for themes in a narrative fashion (Landrum & Garza, 2015). Mixed methodology is often used to corroborate narrative and categorical data (Landrum & Garza, 2015) or to accommodate a wider array of research questions (Kamil, 2004); however, the premise of the study is that there is an identifiable and structured relationship between mindfulness and conflict strategy use between adults in a committed romantic relationship. Qualitative or mixed methods research would not answer the research questions identified by current literature to address the known problem space because the questions require hypothesis testing which is not a part of the qualitative methodology. Therefore, quantitative methodology is the most appropriate for the study given the current empirical research, identified problem space, research questions, and hypotheses.

Rationale for Research Design

The purpose of a quantitative predictive correlational design is to determine if and to what extent change in one variable accounts for the change in a second variable. In the predictive design, prior research is necessary to establish a linear relationship between the variables and it is assumed in the correlational predictive design (Salkind, 2010). Prior research serves not only to establish a statistically significant correlation but also to identify which variable is the predictor and which is to be predicted. A variable is assigned as the predictor variable and another as the criterion variable then analyzed for the degree to which they vary together (Bloomfield & Fisher, 2019). The criterion variable is the one that the literature indicates should change as a result of change in the predictor; however, as noted in Karremans et al. (2017), empirical studies are necessary to support of refute theoretical claims. The literature indicates that traits of mindfulness (predictor) should account for change in the conflict strategy subdomains (criterion), so this study will contribute to the existing literature by providing empirical evidence. Thus, while this topic has been studied in the literature, this study contributes to that existing body of research by addressing limitations and adding empirical research to serve as the basis for making future recommendations. This is also discussed in the problem statement section of Chapter 2. This is a non-experimental study because the variables are not manipulated by the researcher (Salkind, 2010). This aligns with the research questions and hypotheses which were developed to address the identified problem space in the literature.

Quantitative predictive correlational design is the most appropriate for the study. Other quantitative design methodologies include experimental, pre-experimental, quasi-experimental, and comparative. Experimental and quasi-experimental design includes manipulation of variables to determine a casual rather than corollary relationship (Bloomfield & Fisher, 2019). Establishing statistically significant predictive power is necessary prior to dedicating the resources necessary for an experimental or quasi-experimental design. Similarly pre-experimental is inappropriate because there is no proposed intervention to examine the effect of changes in one variable on a second variable (Salkind, 2010). The comparative design describes a study examining differences in a given set of variables across multiple populations (Bloomfield & Fisher, 2019) which does not align with the purpose of the study. Because there is no manipulation of variables or multiple populations, the predictive correlational design most closely aligns with the purpose and research questions of the study.

Population and Sample Selection

The population of interest for this study is adults in a committed romantic relationship. In this study and per the definitions provided in Chapter 1, a committed romantic relationship is defined as one having the characteristics of strong emotional, physical, and sexual attraction with the expectation of and dedication to long-term maintenance. The population of interest refers to the entire group of people to whom the research could appropriately generalize (Lavrakas, 2008). Alternatively, the target population is a subgroup of the population of interest and includes only those people who may be selected for participation in the study (Yang, 2010). The target population for the study is the adults in a committed romantic relationship living in the mid-Atlantic region of the United States who are members of the identified Facebook groups used for recruiting (see Appendix B; combined total of 50,000 people). Because the groups are not only for people in committed romantic relationships, the number of eligible participants in the groups cannot be calculated. The individuals who volunteer to participate in the study are collectively called the study sample (Yang, 2010). Recruitment, sampling strategy, and method for determining the sample size are described below.

Quantitative Sample Size

Appropriate sample size for a quantitative study is essential to avoid type I (false rejection of the null; false positive) and type II (erroneous inability to reject the null; false negative) errors. To determine the appropriate number of participants before the conduction of the study, an a priori (before the study) power analysis is performed using G*Power software. The G*Power software allows the input of statistical test type, alpha, power, and effect size to produce a minimum required sample size. To preserve the statistical power despite multiple hypotheses using the same dataset, the following G*Power analysis includes a Bonferroni correction wherein the alpha coefficient is divided by the number of hypotheses tested (Lee & Lee, 2018) which is 6.

The minimum required sample size was calculated using the power analysis test, G*Power. The G*Power test was set at F tests, linear multiple regression: fixed model, R^2 deviation from zero, a priori: compute required sample size – given alpha, power, and effect size. Linear multiple regression is used for all linear regressions whether simple or multiple, and the number of predictors is changed to align with the research questions which is one. The G*Power analysis was based on the following parameters: effect size = 0.15 (medium), alpha error probability = 0.008 (0.05 / 6), power error probability = 0.80, and number of predictors = 1. The G*Power analysis yielded a minimum of 85 required participants. An additional 13 participants (15%) are added to account for violation of parametric assumptions. There is no need to account for attrition as the informed consent states that incomplete data will not be used; therefore, incomplete responses will be removed, and only complete responses included in the sample. Therefore, at least 98 participants would need to complete the questionnaire to make up an adequate sample given the study parameters.

Recruiting and Sampling Strategy

This study used convenience sampling. Convenience sampling refers to all sampling practices based on cheap and easy access to potential participants despite introduction of selection bias and the danger of having a non-representative sample (Taherdoost, 2016). Due to these limitations, convenience sampling is not appropriate for all research studies. Salkind (2010) notes that convenience sampling is appropriate for a study such as this where the goal is to establish an empirical foundation to support the recommendation to dedicate resources for an experimental study with rigorous sampling methods. Participants were recruited through social media posts on Facebook pages following site approval by the page administration (appendix B) and on the researcher's personal page.

Plan A. The researcher distributed the flyer-like post (see Appendix H) on the approved Facebook sites per the permissions in Appendix B and the researcher's personal Facebook page (approx. 150 members). The combined total participant pool is approximately 50,000 people. Sample size was met (and exceeded) on day 7, the survey was closed, and no further recruitment activities took place.

Facebook yard sale sites provide a geographically specific participant pool. Given that the inclusion criteria specify that a participant must live in the Mid-Atlantic region of the US, it is imperative to target a participant pool specific to that geographic region. Yard sale sites also have very high membership which enable to researcher to target a large participant pool with fewer posts. There are 3 inclusion criteria which are age, location, and relationship status. Location is guaranteed per the requirement of the Facebook pages. Age and relationship status are not; however, the membership is large enough that it is feasible to obtain the needed 98 participants from these groups. The first post was made as soon as IRB approval was received. Per IRB recommendation, the second flyer was used as follow up posts on days 3 and 6 following IRB approval. Plans B and C were not used. Plan B was discouraged by IRB who warned against harassment, so had sample size not been met within 2 weeks (no additional postings in week 2) then the researcher would have proceeded to plan C.

Plan B. The original plan B was to post again three times in week two with the second flyer (see Appendix H); however, IRB discouraged the researcher from posting more than three times to a website to avoid harassment claims. Had sample size not been reached within week one, the researcher would have simply waited for a week with no additional postings. This was not needed as the sample size was met and exceeded at 7 days.

Plan C. If sampling size was not met within 2 weeks of study initiation, then the researcher would have hired the data collection and management company "Qualtrics" to recruit the necessary sample from the target population. Qualtrics® is a paid online data collection service designed to assist researchers reach a target population (Qualtrics, n.d.). While no site authorization is needed to use Qualtrics®, if the service was used then a contract would be secured and signed. This did not prove necessary as sample was reached after 1 week.

The researcher obtained site authorizations by reaching out to the page administrators through Facebook Messenger. When requesting site authorization, the researcher included the purpose statement; researcher's name, affiliation, and contact information; dissertation chair name; and approximate data collection timeline. The researcher reached out to 75 different Facebook yard sale sites, some from each of the five Mid-Atlantic states. Four sites responded with permission to recruit, and they are included as screenshots in Appendix B. According to GCU IRB guidelines, site authorizations are required for any social media site except for the researcher's personal page.

As the purpose of this study was to establish an empirical foundation for future experimental research, the inclusion criteria were left broad. To be eligible, participants must be over 18, in a committed romantic relationship, and currently reside in the mid-Atlantic region of the United States. The development of a Plan A, B, and C recruitment strategy acknowledges the potential challenge of recruiting the required number of participants.

Instrumentation

The proposed research questions require research data on specified traits of mindfulness and romantic partner conflict strategy subdomains as well as additional data for the purpose of creating a profile of the sample. The additional data on sample demographics is not used to answer the research questions; however, related research cites the necessity of acknowledging relevant demographic variables (Harvey et al., 2015). The instruments for collecting research and additional data are described below.

Research Data

Research data refers to information collected for the purpose of answering the research questions. The two featured psychometric tools use Likert scale data which is ordinal in nature as there is not a numerically equal value between each response; however, Likert scale data may be treated as continuous (interval) for the purposes of statistical analysis (Boone & Boone, 2012). Likert scale data is most appropriate to gather data regarding perceptions, attitudes, and feelings (Boone & Boone, 2012) and is therefore most appropriate for the study.

The Five Facet Mindfulness Questionnaire – 15- Item Short Form. The five traits of mindfulness (from the FFMQ) are the predictor variables for the study. The 15-item Five-Facet Mindfulness Questionnaire (FFMQ-15) was used to collect data on the traits of mindfulness and is the short version of the 39-item five facet mindfulness questionnaire. The FFMQ was developed with the goal of capturing the multidimensional nature of mindfulness as a set of dispositions or traits (Baer et al., 2006). The construction is the product of amalgamating traditional Buddhist and contemporary clinical definitions of mindfulness as well as five existing mindfulness self-report measures followed by confirmatory factor analysis (CFA) to ensure appropriate factor loadings (Baer et al., 2006). This publication includes five parts: exploration of psychometric properties of existing measures, exploratory factor analysis identifying five distinct properties of mindfulness (previous measures had a maximum of four), CFA, comparison of five facets with other known related constructs, and testing the validity of the five mindfulness facets to predict mental health symptoms. The FFMQ-15 consists of 15 items selected from the full questionnaire to ensure appropriate construct validity in a shorter form. The 15-item questionnaire was developed and tested using confirmatory factor analysis by Baer et al. (2008) and further validated in Gu et al. (2016) which documented equal internal consistency and external validity as the 39-item questionnaire.

Validity and reliability are detailed in the following sections; however, internal consistency using Cronbach's alpha values range from .75 to .91 (Baer et al., 2006) and validity is demonstrated via sensitivity to change from interventions, integration of traditional and contemporary conceptual definitions, and ability to predict associated mental health symptoms.

The FFMQ-15 includes 5 subscales each with 3 items. The subscales are observing, describing, acting with awareness, nonjudgment of inner experience, and non-reactivity to inner experience. Each item is scored on a scale of 1-5. 1 = never or rarely true, 2 = rarely true, 3 = sometimes true, 4 = often true, or 5 = very often or always true. Therefore, each subscale summative score will range from 3-15. Some items are reverse scored and must be converted prior to calculating the sum score for each subscale. The mean score is used for data analysis, and all mean scores must be between 1 and 5 to be valid. While it is possible to sum the subscale scores for an aggregate score, the subscales are left discrete in this study based on the model and recommendation of relevant literature (see Harvey et al., 2015; Harvey et al., 2019; Karremans et al., 2017). As previously noted, this Likert-scale data will be treated as interval for the purpose of statistical analysis according to the recommendation from Boone and Boone (2012). The Five-Facet Mindfulness Questionnaire is the most appropriate choice for the study due to the inclusion of all recommended facets of mindfulness.

The Romantic Partner Conflict Scale. The Romantic Partner Conflict Scale was designed to address the lack of an available measurement tool to capture typical, day to day conflict interactions between romantic partners. Other available measures capture abusive tendencies or topic specific content such as parenting or finances (Zacchilli et al.,

2009). The initial publication includes 3 studies which detail the development, validity, and reliability of the scale. According to Zacchilli et al. (2009), the scale was initially developed qualitatively, through asking open-ended questions to 18 students in a close relationships undergraduate class then coding the responses for themes. Using the literature, additional items and scales were added to yield a total of 7 scales and 55 items. The scale (along with measures of respect toward partner and relational satisfaction) was administered to 170 participants then refined via confirmatory factor analysis resulting in the 6 scales and 39-items from the preliminary version. The RPCS is the product of research supporting the importance of conflict resolution and management strategies for overall relationship functioning and a lack of available data collection tools (Zacchilli et al., 2009). In the publication, Social Exchange Theory is listed among important theoretical foundations supporting the development of a self-report measure to identify the prevalence of conflict strategies in every day non-abusive romantic partner conflict interactions. The measure was introduced, tested, and validated in a series of studies included in Zacchilli et al. (2009). The final romantic partner scale includes 39-items grouped into 6 conflict strategies which are referred to as subdomains throughout this study.

  The Romantic Partner Conflict Scale (RPCS) evaluates the presence of 6 conflict strategy subdomains during everyday conflict interactions between romantic partners. The strategies serve as the labels for the subscales and the items ask the respondent to identify how much they agree or disagree that a behavior is present during a typical conflict interaction. The behaviors are grouped into strategies per existing literature, confirmatory factor analysis, and existing conflict measures. Therefore, conflict strategies are clusters of behaviors, so the RPCS measures the prevalence of strategies using the prevalence of the behaviors which make up the strategies. For example, one conflict strategy subdomain is compromise. The prevalence of compromise as a strategy is measured by the prevalence of comprising behaviors evidenced through questionnaire items such as, "We try to find solutions that are acceptable to both of us" and "my partner and I negotiate to resolve our disagreements." Participants are asked to self-report how strongly they agree or disagree with the statement thereby indicating the prevalence of comprising conflict strategy during conflict interactions.

The RPCS is a 39-item questionnaire which includes 6 subdomains comprised of items scored on a 5-point Likert-scale ranging from 0-4. 0 = strongly disagree with statement, 1 = moderately disagree with statement, 2 = neutral, neither agree nor disagree, 3 = moderately agree with statement, and 4 = strongly agree with statement. As previously noted, this research data is ordinal, but Boone and Boone (2012) support and recommend treating Likert scale data as continuous (interval) for the purpose of statistical analysis to analyze thoughts, feelings, and perceptions.

There are no reversed scored items, so the means scores from data were calculated without researcher manipulation. The subscales and number of items included for each subscale are compromise – 14 items, avoidance – 3 items, interactional reactivity – 6 items, separation – 5 items, domination – 6 items, and submission – 5 items. The varying number of items for each subscale results in varying total potential summative scores. Although all means scores must be between 0 and 4 to be valid. Additionally, higher scores do not indicate more positive conflict patterns, but greater presence of each type of strategy. Compromise is the only subscale clearly correlated with relationship benefits, while interactional reactivity and domination are solely correlated with negative consequences (Zacchilli et al., 2009). The researchers note that separation, avoidance, and submission are correlated with some positive and some negative consequences precluding their categorization as entirely positive or negative strategies. Despite the lack of clear association with relationship benefits or consequences, the scale has adequate validity and reliability.

The scale measures 6 different conflict strategy subdomains. Discussed in more detail in the next section, the validity of the RPCS is evidenced through factor analysis (subscale averages ranging from .84 to .96) and reliability is documented based on test-retest reliability subscale scores between .70 and .85. Because some are beneficial, some are harmful, and others have mixed relational outcomes, no aggregate score is possible. The data analysis procedures are detailed in a later section of this chapter; however, the proposed data analysis method will yield information on the extent to which each facet of mindfulness predicts each subdomain individually.

Additional Data

Additional data includes information gathered which is not used to answer the research questions. Demographic data is the primary type of additional data and is collected for the purpose of describing the sample as it relates to the identified variables and target population. Another type of additional data, screening questions ensure that respondents meet the established criteria for participation in the study.

Inclusion Criteria. The criteria for participating in the study were age, location, and relationship status. All participants must be over 18 years old, live in the mid-Atlantic region of the US, and be in a committed, romantic relationship. Participants were informed of the inclusion criteria in the recruiting and informed consent information. As age and location are demographic information, participants were asked to select their age from various groupings and any respondents under the age of 18 would have been removed from the study. No respondents selected this response, so none were removed based on age. Participants were asked to select from identified ranges (under 18, 18-25, then in 10-year groupings through 95 years old) to create a profile of the sample. Participants also indicated their state of residence and responses from outside the mid-Atlantic region (Delaware, Maryland, Pennsylvania, Virginia, and West Virginia; see Mid-Atlantic Water Program, 2006) would have been discarded. Again, this was not necessary as all participants selected one of the five identified mid-Atlantic states.

Demographic Questions. Demographic questions serve to create a profile of the sample. Demographic questions included gender, race, length of relationship, education, and previous formal mindfulness training. The demographic questions were developed in part as a response to existing literature suggesting a need for more diversity in age, race, and gender sampling (see Quickert & MacDonald, 2020; Shrout et al., 2020) and research suggesting that demographic variables are relevant for accurate interpretation of study results (Harvey et al., 2015). Length of relationship and education information are collected to create a profile of the sample as it relates to the research variables. The recent research suggests each of these demographic characteristics influence the research variables in a significant way, so it is important to include information on these characteristics when analyzing and explaining the results of the study; however, for each demographic question, the participants had the option to decline to respond. Some of this information may be sensitive to the individual and they may prefer not to self-identify even when personally identifying information is not collected, so participants were permitted to choose whether or not to provide this information.

Validity

This section explores the validity of the measures used to assess the research variables (5 facets of mindfulness and 6 romantic partner conflict strategy subdomains). A primary function of checking the validity of an instrument is to ensure that the measurement tools measure what it claims to measure (Beck, 2020). Validity is 'the truth, the whole truth, and nothing but the truth', and includes the precision of the measurement tool to capture only the entire essence of the specific construct it purports to measure in terms of construct, concept, and criterion. Concept validity is the degree to which the assessment tool aligns with the theoretical understanding while construct validity refers to the accurate operationalization of the idea into measurable dimensions (Weiner, 2001). These items are typically reviewed by content experts. Criterion validity is the ability of a measurement tool to correctly filter respondents (positives participants are identified as positive by the assessment, negative participants are identified as negative) and is measured by comparing the results of the assessment in question to other, established assessments (Lin et al., 2019). Establishing the validity of a measurement tool is a timely and necessary process. To ensure verbatim duplication of all items for the measurements tools and permission to use them, both the original questionnaire and the questionnaire given to participants is included as appendix E.

The validity of the Five Facet Mindfulness Questionnaire has been established both in its full-length version and its various shortened forms. The 39-item questionnaire was developed and tested in a series of five studies published by Baer et al. (2006). Study one reviewed the psychometrics of available mindfulness measures and noted significant variance in association with other constructs such as mental health symptoms and emotional intelligence. This indicated a need for redefining mindfulness leading to study two which details the exploration of mindfulness facets by conducting exploratory factor analysis and correlational analyses on data from 613 participants who completed the five mindfulness measures from study one. This led to the development of a new definition of mindfulness which includes five facets. Previous mindfulness measures had a maximum of four dimensions. Study three is confirmatory factor analysis which is discussed in the reliability section. Study four compared the five identified facets of mindfulness with other known related constructs from traditional and contemporary mindfulness literature. The FFMQ (differentially between facets) was positively correlated with emotional intelligence and self-compassion, and negatively correlated with dissociation and thought suppression which aligns with both traditional and contemporary literature. This establishes concept validity. Incremental validity is established in study five wherein three of the five traits (acting with awareness, non-reactivity, and non-judging) account for a greater statistical portion of the variance in well-being than do the other existing measures.

This study used the 15-item version of the questionnaire which was developed by Baer et al. (2008) by extracting 15 items from the original 39-item version and conducting CFA to ensure psychometric consistency. To establish criterion validity for the shortened version of the FFMQ, results of the FFMQ-15 are negatively correlated with symptoms depression and anxiety and positively correlated with measures of well-being (Meng et al., 2020) which corresponds to other research on mindfulness and mental health symptoms. Gu et al. (2016) first highlights the validity of the 39 – item full length questionnaire then compares results from the 39 and 15-item questionnaire to support the 15-item version as a valid measurement tool. Meng et al. (2020) also provided validation for the 15-item version of the FFMQ as a valid measurement for working adults and cited the utility of a valid short form for use when the full-length version may present participant burden.

Reviewing the five-facet mindfulness structure more generally, Karl and Fischer (2020) compare the facets of the FFMQ to several other accepted mindfulness measures to explore the construct and concept validity of the FFMQ. According to Karl and Fischer (2020) the FFMQ has a few significant conceptual differences attributable to its greater emphasis of Eastern mindfulness principles which does not decrease the concept validity but is important to note. Three facets (observing, describing, and acting with awareness) are supported as distinct constructs while two (nonjudging and non-reactivity) were often merged in other mindfulness assessments suggesting potential overlap in the behavioral and cognitive activities captured by these items (Karl & Fischer, 2020). Harvey et al. (2015) specifically cites absence of the non-reactivity scale as a limitation to the study while Harvey et al. (2019) cites the need to include a non-judging dimension. There are notable distinctions between the FFMQ and other accepted mindfulness measures due to the different theoretical foundations; however, both the full version and the 15-item FFMQ have acceptable levels of concept, construct, and criterion validity.

The RPCS is not so widely used as the FFMQ and therefore fewer validation studies exist. The original article published by Zacchilli et al. in 2009 contains three research studies for exploratory factor analysis, confirmatory factor analysis, and test-retest reliability. Exploratory factor analysis was based on 55 items developed from qualitative interviews and themes in the literature then items were removed for complexity, or improper factor loadings leaving 39 items organized into 6 subscales. Factor loadings varied from .53 to .88. Items were dropped if they did not load highly enough (at least .4) on any one factor or if they loaded highly on more than one factor.

The confirmatory factor analysis confirmed the items from study one adding to the construct validity and provided information related to criterion validity by correlating subscale measures to constructs including established conflict measures, relationship satisfaction, respect, sexual communication, love styles, and self-disclosure (Zacchilli et al., 2009). Study two provides information related to the categorization of subscale concepts as either positive or negative based on the effects of the conflict strategy on the relationship. The only consistently positive conflict strategy identified by the scale is compromise. Harmful conflict strategies include domination and interactional reactivity. As previously noted, separation, avoidance, and submission are not exclusively associated with either benefits or consequences indicating nuanced interplay with other relationship factors. For the purpose of this study, separation, avoidance, and submission are referred to as uncategorized. The study included several protections to ensure appropriate validity.

In addition to the three studies published in 2009 by the researchers who developed the scale, other researchers have used the measure which provides additional information regarding validity. Fiserova et al. (2021) cites translation and validation of the RPCS in Czechoslovakian. Harvey et al. (2015) and Harvey et al. (2019) both feature the RPCS as the measurement tool for romantic partner conflict. While Harvey et al.

(2019) does not specifically discuss the validity of the RPCS, the scale is discussed, and clearly aligns, with contemporary research on romantic partner conflict interactions and strategies. This increases the concept and construct validity of the RPCS. It is also important to note that while the mindfulness measure is noted as a limitation of Harvey et al. (2015) and Harvey et al. (2019), the RPCS is not. Harvey et al. (2015) cites the focus of the RPCS on day-to-day conflict (rather than abusive or topic-specific conflict) as a primary motivator for selecting it as the conflict measure. This aligns with the purpose and scope of the study as typical, routine conflict interactions is also the present focus. Selecting a measurement tool that precisely measures the identified variable is an important dimension of validity. A measurement tool used for abusive relationships or content-specific conflict (e.g., parenting or finances) would not be appropriate.

There are internal and external factors which threaten the validity of research data. Instrument validity is the accuracy of a tool to measure what it claims to measure which informs the accuracy of the inferences drawn as a result of the study (Beck, 2020). The steps taken to ensure appropriate validity include exact duplication of high-quality instruments, adequate sample size (including a Bonferroni correction for repeated testing), precise and clear participant inclusion criteria, proper data cleaning procedures, and statistical testing to ensure the data are appropriate for linear regression analysis. To limit threats to validity due to sampling characteristics, the inclusion criteria are clearly stated on the recruitment post, the informed consent, and participants are required to confirm demographics once the survey begins. The Bonferroni correction increased the required sample size to adjust for the repeated use of the same data in statistical analysis which decreases the probably of an inaccurately rejected null hypothesis. To guard against internal threats to power and validity, an a priori power analysis using G*Power with a Bonferroni correction determined the needed sample size (see Appendix F). Additionally, if the hypothesis testing demonstrated that the data are not appropriate for a parametric then the proposal was to use Siegel estimator instead (see Data Analysis Procedures for more detail). If the study is found invalid by power analysis or statistical procedures, then it will be deemed not generalizable, and the reasons noted in the limitations section of Chapter 4. In addition to validity, reliability is an important consideration because it defines the generalizability of the study.

Reliability

Reliability is the term for the internal and external consistency of an assessment. Internal reliability, measured using Cronbach's alpha, is a measure of how similar the scores are for similar items (Jansen et al., 2021) and Cronbach scores range from 0 – 1 where scores from 0.6 to 0.8 are considered moderate and acceptable (Meng et al., 2020). Logically, different items measuring a similar construct should be scored similarly by the same respondent; However, an item with a low Cronbach score may be retained if it is deemed necessary for validity (Jansen et al., 2021). External consistency is often referred to as test-retest reliability. In de Assis et al. (2008) test-retest reliability is defined as the consistency of reports across timespans or between similar respondents. Both require multiple uses of the same assessment and are therefore a timely but necessary process.

Several studies have explored and verified the internal and external reliability of the FFMQ full version, and the 15-item version used in this study. Baer et al. (2006) cites Cronbach alpha scores ranging from .75 - .91 during the initial development of the full-length questionnaire. Meng et al. (2020) cite the correlation between the full version and the 15-item short form as verified and significant (correlation =.70 and significant at p<0.05) thereby supporting the reliability of the short version. The test-retest consistency is explored and verified in Gu et al. (2016) in which the 39 and 15 item FFMQ is administered pre and post MBCT intervention. The FFMQ-15 is determined as reliable and sensitive to change in the individual. Therefore, the FFMQ-15 is acceptably reliable on internal and external measures.

The reliability information for the RPCS primarily consists of Cronbach alpha scores and test-retest reliability. Published in the initial development study, Cronbach alpha scores for each subscale are .96 for compromise, .91 for domination, .88 for submission, .89 for separation, .84 for avoidance, and .88 for interactional reactivity (Zacchilli et al., 2009). Using data gathered in another study, Harvey et al. (2015) published Cronbach scores of .82 for avoidance, .91 for compromise, .81 for interactional reactivity, .88 for submission, .88 for separation, and .90 for domination. Regarding test-retest reliability, study three published in Zacchilli et al. (2009) cites correlations between .70 to .85 for each subscale when the assessment is administered to the same respondents one month apart. With each use of the RPCS in empirical literature, the reliability data grows. This study will add to the growing body of literature documenting the reliability of the RPCS to measure every day romantic partner conflict strategies.

As with validity, measures are in place to safeguard and verify the reliability of the study. First, the featured measurement tools have existing evidence to support appropriate internal and external reliability. Second, the researcher ensured exact duplication of these study instruments. Third, the internal reliability is confirmed using statistical calculation of Cronbach's alpha. No testing of external reliability (test-retest) is possible given that the participants only complete the survey one time. Any deficits in reliability are noted in the limitations section of Chapter 4.

Data Collection and Management

The first necessary steps for data collection are site, quality review and IRB approvals. Per GCU IRB policy, site approval were obtained from the administrators of each Facebook page used for recruitment (Appendix B) except the researcher's personal page. After the research proposal was approved by all members of the dissertation committee, the proposal was sent to quality review for revisions and approval. After quality review, an application was submitted to and approved by the IRB (Appendix C) followed by participant recruitment. Participants were recruited through Facebook posts on the approved pages. The post was a flyer-type image with information about the study, participant requirements, the SurveyMonkey link, and the researcher's contact information for questions about the questionnaire or study. The posts were made shareable so they could be forwarded to other interested people.

Once participants were recruited, the next step was data collection. The SurveyMonkey link in the recruitment post took the participant directly to a welcome page to assure participants that they were on the correct webpage. The welcome page was followed by the informed consent page. Following the welcome page, the informed consent (Appendix D) was the first item available to potential participants and must have been confirmed prior to beginning the questionnaire. Information contained within the informed consent included a brief description of the study, participant requirements, any anticipated potential risks or benefits, people with access to the questionnaire results, researcher contact information, data security measures, and possible future research. A question at the end asked a participant if they meet the requirements and would like to participate. They selected "I agree" or "I do not agree." If the participant selected 'I agree' then they were permitted access to the second page of the questionnaire; however, if they select 'I do not agree' then they would have been directed to an exit screen and not permitted access to the rest of the questionnaire. Based on the SurveyMonkey results, no participant selected 'I do not agree', so all participants continued to the second page of the questionnaire.

The second page of the questionnaire had the demographic items, and each page after that had 10 survey questions which was 54 questions spread across 6 survey pages (15 questions from the FFMQ-15 first then 39 questions from the RPCS). The final page of the questionnaire was a thank you page confirming submission of the questionnaire. Both the disqualification and thank you page included the researcher's name, email address, and phone number for any participant questions.

The three types of data collected from participants were demographic, RPCS, and FFMQ-15. All demographic questions not required to confirm inclusion criteria had a 'prefer not to answer' option to preserve participant comfort. To maintain anonymity, no identifying information was collected, and the respondents were assigned an identifying number based on survey completion (the first completed response is identified as 1, the second as 2, and so forth). Any respondents indicating age below 18 years old or a state outside the mid-Atlantic region of the US would have automatically been redirected to the disqualification end screen and not permitted to continue to the survey instruments. This featured was not utilized as no participants made those selections.

Each participant has 7 demographic responses, 6 subscale scores for the RPCS, and 5 subscale scores for the FFMQ-15. The subscale scores are the mean for all items assigned to a given subscale. Each subscale in the FFMQ-15 has 3 items with Likert-scale ratings of 1-5; therefore, each score should be between 1 and 5. The number of items in the subscales for the RPCS vary greatly; however, the mean score for each subscale should be between 0 and 4 as the Likert-scale for the RPCS goes from 0 to 4. The scale measures the presence of strategies, and each subscale measures the presence of a different conflict strategy or subdomain. All subscales are used individually to answer each research question as an aggregate score is not possible per the instrument guidelines.

The questionnaire remained open until complete data collection from at least 98 participants was complete. The data were downloaded from SurveyMonkey into an excel spreadsheet for cleaning and analysis. The data is stored on the researcher's password protected laptop and a thumb drive to prevent data loss. The thumb drive is stored in a locked safe at the researcher's home. The data from the thumb drive and laptop will be permanently deleted 3 years after the conclusion of the research.

Data Analysis Procedures

The purpose of this quantitative predictive correlational study was to determine if and to what extent the five mechanisms of mindfulness identified in the Five Facet Mindfulness Questionnaire predict the six conflict strategy subdomains identified in the Romantic Partner Conflict Scale used by adults in a committed romantic relationship living in the mid-Atlantic region of the United States. This section is a thorough discussion of the complete set of data analysis procedures used in this study. The purpose of data analysis is to use the sample data to address the identified research questions. The identified research questions and corresponding hypotheses for this study are

- RQ1: Does acting with awareness predict conflict strategy subdomains used between adults in a committed romantic relationship?

- H_o1: Acting with awareness does not predict conflict strategy use between adults in a committed romantic relationship for the following subdomains:
    - Compromise
    - Avoidance
    - Interactional Reactivity
    - Separation
    - Domination
    - Submission

- H_a1: Acting with awareness predicts conflict strategy use between adults in a committed romantic relationship for the following subdomains:
    - Compromise
    - Avoidance
    - Interactional Reactivity
    - Separation
    - Domination
    - Submission

- RQ2: Does observing predict conflict strategy subdomains used between adults in a committed romantic relationship?

H_o2: Observing does not predict conflict strategy use between adults in a committed romantic relationship for the following subdomains:

- Compromise
- Avoidance
- Interactional Reactivity
- Separation
- Domination
- Submission

H_a2: Observing predicts conflict strategy use between adults in a committed romantic relationship for the following subdomains:

- Compromise
- Avoidance
- Interactional Reactivity
- Separation
- Domination
- Submission

RQ3: Does describing predict conflict strategy subdomains used between adults in a committed romantic relationship?

H_o3: Describing does not predict conflict strategy use between adults in a committed romantic relationship for the following subdomains:

- Compromise
- Avoidance
- Interactional Reactivity

- Separation
- Domination
- Submission

H_a3: Describing predicts conflict strategy use between adults in a committed romantic relationship for the following subdomains:

- Compromise
- Avoidance
- Interactional Reactivity
- Separation
- Domination
- Submission

RQ4: Does non-judging predict conflict strategy subdomains used between adults in a committed romantic relationship?

H_o4: Non-judging does not predict conflict strategy use between adults in a committed romantic relationship for the following subdomains:

- Compromise
- Avoidance
- Interactional Reactivity
- Separation
- Domination
- Submission

H_a4: Non-judging predicts conflict strategy use between adults in a committed romantic relationship for the following subdomains:

- Compromise
- Avoidance
- Interactional Reactivity
- Separation
- Domination
- Submission

RQ5: Does non-reactivity predict conflict strategy subdomains used in conflict interactions between adults in a committed romantic relationship?

H_o5: Non-reactivity does not predict conflict strategy use between adults in a committed romantic relationship for the following subdomains:
- Compromise
- Avoidance
- Interactional Reactivity
- Separation
- Domination
- Submission

H_a5: Non-reactivity predicts conflict strategy use between adults in a committed romantic relationship for the following subdomains:
- Compromise
- Avoidance
- Interactional Reactivity
- Separation
- Domination

- Submission

The data analysis procedures include all the steps required for appropriate and accurate use of the scored data to complete statistical analysis and answer the identified research questions. All data organizing, cleaning, and analysis occurred within SPSS. The steps include importing data to SPSS organizing and cleaning the data in SPSS, calculating subscale and overall scores in SPSS, and using SPSS to complete descriptive statistical analysis, testing assumptions, and inferential statistical analysis.

Organizing and Cleaning

The first step is to transfer all the raw sample data into SPSS. The data were downloaded directly from SurveyMonkey into SPSS. Each participant's data is marked by the number corresponding to response completion. Responses indicating violation of participation criteria were discarded prior to assigning completion numbers. Based on the recommendation of Kwak and Kim (2017), any missing values would be substituted with the average subscale value. For example, if a response was missing an item value under an item for the non-judging subscale of the FFMQ-15 then the researcher would calculate the mean subscale score and input that score for the missing value. Data cleaning procedures include checking for data entry and measurement errors and using a scatterplot to check for outliers and abnormal values. Any identified data entry errors were corrected. Outliers and abnormal values were reviewed and an explanation for the value or rationale for removal would be provided in Chapter 4. Identification of errors would require adjusted values, elimination of errors from the assessment, and a re-test for outliers. To ensure only eligible participants complete the survey, the inclusion criteria were stated on the recruitment flyer and must be acknowledged by the participant as part of the informed consent.

Descriptive Statistical Analysis

Participant data including demographic data, RPCS subscale scores, and FFMQ-15 subscale scores were transferred into a SPSS sheet by the researcher and reviewed for accuracy. Descriptive statistics are ways of simplifying and organizing data to provide a visual summary of the data distribution (Gravetter & Wallnau, 2020). Descriptive statistics used to describe the research variables (5 traits of mindfulness and 6 conflict strategy subdomains) include mean, minimum and maximum scores, variance, standard deviation, skewness, and kurtosis. Frequency and percent are used to represent the demographic data (age, gender, race, type of relationship, length of relationship, formal mindfulness training, education, and religion). The descriptive data demonstrate the demographic and research data characteristics of the 103-participant sample in both numerical and graphical displays. This can be found in Chapter 4. The SPSS output charts are added under Appendix I.

Scale Reliability

Scale reliability is measured and demonstrated using Cronbach's alpha. Cronbach's alpha is a measure of internal consistency to determine reliability of scales for Likert questions in Surveys (Laerd Statistics, 2018a). The Cronbach's alpha scores derived from this study's data set are compared to those of the developers and previous research studies to provide an indication of this study's internal reliability. The Cronbach's alpha scores are calculated from the data to offer an assessment of the internal consistency for each of the instrument scales.

Testing Assumptions

Prior to completion of inferential statistical analysis, it is imperative to determine if the data are parametric or nonparametric because this will inform the type of statistical test used. Typically resulting in greater power, parametric tests are preferred (Salkind, 2010); however, it requires that certain assumptions about the data are met. The assumptions for running a parametric test differ based on the statistical analysis. The assumptions discussed in this section are specific to using a parametric test for linear regression analysis. According to Laerd Statistics (2018c) the six assumptions that must be met for parametric linear regression analysis to be appropriate are that variables must be continuous, there must be a linear relationship between the variables, no significant outliers may exist, the variables must exist in independent observation, homoscedasticity, and the data must conform to a normal distribution.

The first assumption requires that the variable be continuous (i.e., interval or ratio); however, the research variables are measured using Likert-scales which yield ordinal scale data. It is recommended to treat Likert-scale data as interval for the purposes of data analysis using a linear regression analysis (Boone & Boone, 2012). After data collection, the requirement that the variables exist in a linear relationship was tested in SPSS using a scatterplot to graphically demonstrate the relationship between the variables. This is a crucial assumption for parametric linear regression analysis (Ernst & Albers, 2017), so if violated then the Siegel Estimator non-parametric regression is proposed to be used in place of parametric linear regression analysis. The third assumption requires there be no significant outliers which can significantly alter the strength and even direction of the correlation (Laerd Statistics, 2018c2018c). Some causes of outliers include data entry mistakes, errors in data collection (participants select an erroneous score), or entry of an invalid response. Other outliers are simply valid participant responses that are greater than 2 standard deviations away from the mean. A boxplot is used to identify any existing outliers. The outliers were reviewed to determine the cause and removed if they are errors. If they are not errors and the outlier significantly alters the strengths or direction of the correlation, then this would constitute a violation of the assumptions for a parametric linear regression analysis.

Also, in SPSS and following data collection, independence was tested and verified through the use of the Durbin-Watson statistic. The Durbin-Watson statistic is the most common test for identifying the presence of autocorrelation and yields a score between 0 and 4 where values close to 2 indicate independence (Turner et al., 2021). Violations of this assumption are severe and would require the use of a nonparametric test (Ernst & Albers, 2017). which for this study would be the Siegel Estimator. Homoscedasticity is demonstrated using a scatterplot. Based on the recommendation from Laerd Statistics (2018f) the same scatterplot is used to test for homoscedasticity and a linear relationship. The shape of the scatterplot will be identified as either spread evenly, fanned, or funneled. Fan or funnel shaped data violates the assumption of homoscedasticity by representing heteroscedastic data (Laerd Statistics, 2018c). Ernst and Albers (2017) endorse the use of a parametric linear regression analysis even if there is a violation of the homoscedasticity assumption. The sixth and final assumption requires that the residuals conform to a normal distribution. A P-P plot is a graph used to visually identify whether or not the distribution of residuals is normal enough to justify a parametric analysis using linear regression. If this assumption is violated, then the Siegel

Estimator non-parametric regression would be used in place of the parametric linear regression analysis.

With the exception of the homoscedasticity assumption per the recommendation of Ernst and Albers (2017), if the parametric test assumptions are violated then the Siegel Estimator non-parametric regression could be used in its place. A parametric linear regression analysis is preferred because nonparametric testing may have less power to assess significance in relationships (Ali & Bhaskar, 2016). There are three assumptions for a nonparametric test which uses the Siegel estimator in place of linear regression. The three assumptions are: continuous or ordinal variables, two variables representing a paired observation, and the existence of a monotonic relationship (Laerd Statistics, 2018e). The results of the assumptions tests will determine whether parametric or non-parametric tests are most appropriate given the data structure.

Testing Research Hypotheses

If no assumptions were violated, then inferential statistical analysis would have been completed using linear regression analysis to test the research hypotheses and answer the research questions. This study proposed five research questions. All questions require linear regression to identify if and to what extent change in each facet of mindfulness (from the FFMQ) predicts change in the use of 6 conflict strategy subdomains (from the RPCS). The results are discussed in chapter 4.

Linear regression yields the statistics needed to answer the research questions. The results are used to either reject or fail to reject the null hypothesis for each question. As part of calculating linear regression, it is necessary to first calculate the correlation coefficient which is included in the discussion but not used to answer the research questions. Pearson's *r* is used to determine the presence, direction, and strength of a relationship between two variables by comparing the actual data points to the line of best fit (Laerd Statistics, 2018d). The correlation varies from -1.0 to +1.0 where $r = -1.0$ is a perfect negative relationship, $r = 0$ is no relationship, and $r = +1.0$ is a perfect positive relationship (Laerd Statistics, 2018d). Pearson's *r* correlation does not answer the research questions because there is no predictive power; however, Pearson's *r* is a necessary precursor to linear regression analysis and is calculated automatically when using SPSS to conduct linear regression analysis.

A linear regression was proposed to test all the research hypotheses. A linear regression is the next logical step after a correlation and is used to determine the predictive power of one variable for another (Laerd Statistics, 2018c) which was the purpose of the study. The linear regression analysis yields the information required to identify if and to what extent the change in each facet of mindfulness (identified in the FFMQ) predicts the change in the use of the 6 conflict strategy subdomains (identified in the RPCS). Laerd Statistics (2018c) identifies the predictive power as the R-squared value which is the variation in the criterion variable as a result of change in the predictor variable. Therefore, the R-squared value for this study is the total amount of variation in conflict strategy use that is explained by variance in each trait of mindfulness. As the name suggests, the linear regression R-squared value is determined by calculating the square of the Pearson's *r* coefficient.

After verifying that the regression assumptions are met, the researcher would run the standard linear regression in SPSS. The regression would have been run 30 times as there are five different predictor variables (the five facets of mindfulness identified in the

FFMQ) and 6 criterion variables (the subdomains identified in the RPCS). The steps for conducting a linear regression analysis in SPSS are

1. Open SPSS, manually enter and review data (discussed previously)
2. Verify assumptions are met for parametric linear regression analysis (discussed previously)
3. Select Analyze then Regression then Linear.
4. Transfer first predictor variable to the 'Independent(s)' box and first of six conflict strategy subdomains (criterion variable) to the 'Dependent(s)' box
5. Retain all default settings including estimates, model fit, confidence interval set at 95% then run the regression.
6. Repeat steps 3-5 for each predictor and each criterion.

Once the regression is run then SPSS generates a series of tables including goodness of fit, R and R-Squared values, and statistical significance of the predictor variable. The predictors that yield a p value less than .008 will be considered significant and the null hypothesis is rejected. The significance of each regression analysis is used to reject or fail to reject the null hypothesis. There are 6 hypotheses for each of the 5 research questions.

The results of the assumptions testing, and data analysis are detailed in Chapter 4. The demographic data, research data, and assumptions testing are detailed using both visual representation and written narrative. The tables generated by SPSS are used to conclude if and to what extent the five mechanisms of mindfulness identified in the Five Facet Mindfulness Questionnaire predict the six conflict strategy subdomains identified in the Romantic Partner Conflict Scale used by adults in a committed romantic relationship living in the mid-Atlantic region of the United States. Each of the five facets of mindfulness are discussed separately and the ability or failure to reject the null hypothesis is based on the p value which is the probability that the statistical values occurred by chance rather than as a result of the relationship between the variables. A p value greater than .008 constitutes failure to reject the null hypothesis. A failure to reject the null hypothesis is interpreted as the inability to conclude that the predictor accounts for a statistically significant level of change in the criterion variable. Chapter 4 includes detailed visual and narrative evidence to support or reject the null hypotheses.

Ethical Considerations

According to the Belmont Report, all human subjects research must adhere to the principles of respect, justice, and beneficence. Compliance to all aspects of these principles was reviewed and confirmed by the IRB assigned to this study. IRB approval was obtained prior to any participant recruitment or data collection. Approval to commence recruitment and data collection is contingent upon review of the ethical nature of the informed consent procedure, privacy and security measures, the absence of coercion and conflict of interest, and overall data management and analysis procedures.

All aspects of the research must adhere to the principles of respect, justice, and beneficence. Respect refers to the protection of participants' autonomy which includes a comprehensive informed consent process prior to participation and the ability for participants to exit the study at any time without negative consequence. Respect also includes the participants' right to know the purpose and use of their data, to be ensured of appropriate confidentiality, and to be free from coercion. All of this information is included in the informed consent which is required prior to participation in the study. Participants were informed that the researcher, IRB, committee members, peer reviewers, and doctoral college representatives all have access to the raw data. Confidentiality is assured through the collection of personal data only in the form of the identified demographic information which participants were able to decline to answer with the exception of those questions required to confirm inclusion criteria. Raw data is secured on a password protected thumb drive, password protected laptop, or locked safe for at least three years following the conclusion of the study.

Beneficence is the principle of maximized benefits and minimized risk of harm to participants. While there is potential for this study to be used to benefit the target population, there are no direct benefits to participants as a result of participation in the study. There are no physical risks to participants and little risk of mental distress; however, there was potential for participants to feel some psychological discomfort as a result of questions related to romantic partner conflict. There was a disclaimer in the informed consent that the questionnaire includes some questions that may cause discomfort to participants and participants were encouraged to discontinue the questionnaire if it became distressing for them.

Justice is the ethical principle that all benefits and costs should be equally available to all participants and that all procedures be reasonable and non-exploitive. This directly relates to any potential conflicts of interest or coercion. There was no risk of coercion as the researcher has no knowledge of who has or has not participated in the study nor were there any incentives offered for participation. There were no conflicts of interest to report. Justice also often refers to the inclusion of minority groups including sexual minorities which are frequently under-represented in romantic relationship research. Sexual minorities were consciously included in the development of the demographic questionnaire through availability of a host of gender options in addition to an 'other' option.

Assumptions and Delimitations

The quality of the conclusions from any research study depends not only on the validity and reliability of the measurement tools used, but also on the actual process used to recruit participants and those used to collect and to analyze the data. Assumptions are aspects of the population or procedures which the researcher (and potential reader) accepts to be true or at least plausible (Lewis-Beck et al., 2004). Often assumptions are either likely to be true or things that the researcher cannot control, such as the truthfulness of participants in a self-report survey. Delimitations are the choices made by the researcher to identify, clarify, and narrow the focus of the research study (McGregor, 2018). Delimitations are an inherent part of any study and serve to keep the study from becoming too large and unmanageable. Delimitations should align with the purpose of the study and have a basis in existing empirical literature. Both assumptions and delimitations affect the generalizability and applicability of the study and therefore must be a conscious area of focus for the researcher. The assumptions should be logical or unavoidable and the delimitations should align with the purpose statement for the study.

Assumptions

Inherent in the use of self-report measures is the assumption of true and accurate responses by participants. Incorrect responses by participants whether from intentional deception or lack of insight would result in inaccurate results that would not generalize to the target population. Another assumption is that the RPCS and FFMQ-15 are valid and reliable measurements for the current romantic partner conflict strategy use and trait mindfulness of participants. This is only a partial assumption due to the availability of some validity and reliability evidence as previously discussed. It is also assumed that participants followed all instructions provided in the informed consent including not sharing responses with other participants. Sharing responses or discussing items during completion is likely to influence the responses and therefore alter the validity and reliability.

Delimitations

Delimitations include all theoretical and methodological choices made by the researcher. Choices include variables, theoretical foundation, research questions, participant inclusion and exclusion criteria, and data analysis procedures. For maximum generalizability and applicability all decisions must align with each other and with the problem and purpose statements. Any misalignment in theoretical and methodological decisions by the researcher decreases the overall value of the study. The first choice is the variables chosen for study which is the result of research and personal experience of the researcher.

The theoretical foundations were selected through careful review of the measurement tools frequently used to measure the identified variables in other empirical studies. The measurement tools (RPCS and FFMQ-15) were selected based on alignment with the purpose of the study and the availability of validity and reliability information. The FFMQ-15 was also selected to satisfy a recommendation in the literature that mindfulness be measured as more than simply attention (Harvey et al., 2019). The FFMQ-15 is based primarily on the mindfulness model developed by Jon Kabat-Zinn while the RPCS cites social exchange theory as a primary guiding theoretical framework. The research questions were selected to address information missing in existing empirical literature and the data analysis procedures were developed to address the research questions most effectively.

The participant inclusion and exclusion criteria are the result of logic and necessity. There may be inherent differences in the variable presentation for adolescents versus adults, individuals in committed relationships versus more casual relationships or even no relationship, and for individuals in various geographic areas. There may also be variation based on religious background, education, socioeconomic status, racial/cultural/ethnic background, disability status, sexual and gender minority status, mental health status, trauma history, relationship history, or previous formal mindfulness training. The current study is a pilot study to explore preliminary predictive power, so the inclusion criteria are intentionally broad. Alterations in study delimitations for future research is discussed in the recommendations section.

Summary

Methodology refers to all choices and procedures required to plan, run, and discuss a research study. It is essential that all parts of a research study are aligned meaning that rationale and execution are congruent. Therefore, the purpose of chapter 3 is to detail how the methodological decisions align from rationale through execution and discussion. The quantitative methodology and predictive correlational design is most appropriate for use when there is a statistical and identifiable 'truth' to be discovered (Tuli, 2011). The empirically supported research questions contain hypotheses which are the 'truth' to be discovered. To ensure that the results will yield the appropriate power, an a priori G*Power analysis was conducted including a Bonferroni correction and added 15% for potential violation of parametric assumptions yielding a required 98 participants with completed responses. The participants are voluntary members of the target population which is a subset of the population and represents all people will the opportunity to participant in the study. The target population is a delimitation based on logic and necessity as well as recommendations from empirical literature.

The target population is adults in a committed romantic relationship living in the mid-Atlantic region of the United States who are members of the Facebook groups in which the researcher will post the recruitment flyer. The sample, all people who completed the study, are volunteers recruited through a flyer-like shareable post on selected and approved Facebook pages (see Appendix B). After acknowledging the informed consent, the participants completed the demographic questions and the research instruments. The instruments are the five-facet mindfulness questionnaire – 15 item short form, and the romantic partner conflict scale. The raw data is organized and cleaned to allow for statistical analysis. The demographic data is used to ensure participants meet the inclusion criteria and to create a profile of the sample. The plan is that all research questions are answered by using linear regression to determine the extent to which changes in facets of mindfulness predict changes in the use of the conflict strategy subdomains identified in the RPCS. Violations of parametric assumptions would require a change in statistical test for data analysis.

The methodological choices laid out in chapter 3 align with the problem space identified in the literature and detailed in chapters 1 and 2. The purpose of this study is to meaningfully address a missing element in existing literature by providing sufficient evidence on mindfulness as a predictor of romantic partner conflict strategies. The remaining sections of this dissertation include the data analysis and discussion chapters.

Chapter 4 details the data analysis procedures and presents the results using tables and charts. The results include the actual data collected from the participants, the cleaning and preparation of the data, the statistical analysis, followed by the presentation of the results. The results should be the R-squared values derived from the linear regression which leads to the rejection or failure to reject the null hypothesis for each research question.

Chapter 4: Data Analysis and Results

Introduction

The purpose of this quantitative predictive correlational study was to determine if and to what extent the five mechanisms of mindfulness identified in the Five Facet Mindfulness Questionnaire predict the six conflict strategy subdomains identified in the Romantic Partner Conflict Scale used by adults in a committed romantic relationship living in the mid-Atlantic region of the United States. Thus far, a review of existing literature and theoretical foundations supports a positive influence of mindfulness on romantic partner conflict strategies; however, this quantitative predictive correlational study proposed the following research hypotheses to address the current gap in empirical literature.

RQ1: Does acting with awareness predict conflict strategy subdomains used between adults in a committed romantic relationship?

H_o1: Acting with awareness does not predict conflict strategy use between adults in a committed romantic relationship for the following subdomains:

- Compromise
- Avoidance
- Interactional Reactivity
- Separation
- Domination
- Submission

H_a1: Acting with awareness predicts conflict strategy use between adults in a committed romantic relationship for the following subdomains:

- o Compromise
- o Avoidance
- o Interactional Reactivity
- o Separation
- o Domination
- o Submission

RQ2: Does observing predict conflict strategy subdomains used between adults in a committed romantic relationship?

H_o2: Observing does not predict conflict strategy use between adults in a committed romantic relationship for the following subdomains:

- o Compromise
- o Avoidance
- o Interactional Reactivity
- o Separation
- o Domination
- o Submission

H_a2: Observing predicts conflict strategy use between adults in a committed romantic relationship for the following subdomains:

- o Compromise
- o Avoidance
- o Interactional Reactivity
- o Separation
- o Domination

- Submission

RQ3: Does describing predict conflict strategy subdomains used between adults in a committed romantic relationship?

H_o3: Describing does not predict conflict strategy use between adults in a committed romantic relationship for the following subdomains:

- Compromise
- Avoidance
- Interactional Reactivity
- Separation
- Domination
- Submission

H_a3: Describing predicts conflict strategy use between adults in a committed romantic relationship for the following subdomains:

- Compromise
- Avoidance
- Interactional Reactivity
- Separation
- Domination
- Submission

RQ4: Does non-judging predict conflict strategy subdomains used between adults in a committed romantic relationship?

H_o4: Non-judging does not predict conflict strategy use between adults in a committed romantic relationship for the following subdomains:

- Compromise
- Avoidance
- Interactional Reactivity
- Separation
- Domination
- Submission

H_a4: Non-judging predicts conflict strategy use between adults in a committed romantic relationship for the following subdomains:

- Compromise
- Avoidance
- Interactional Reactivity
- Separation
- Domination
- Submission

RQ5: Does non-reactivity predict conflict strategy subdomains used in conflict interactions between adults in a committed romantic relationship?

H_o5: Non-reactivity does not predict conflict strategy use between adults in a committed romantic relationship for the following subdomains:

- Compromise
- Avoidance
- Interactional Reactivity
- Separation
- Domination

- Submission

H_a5: Non-reactivity predicts conflict strategy use between adults in a committed romantic relationship for the following subdomains:

- Compromise
- Avoidance
- Interactional Reactivity
- Separation
- Domination
- Submission

This chapter is a detailed account of all relevant changes to the proposal, data preparation and analysis steps, and findings from the descriptive and statistical analysis. The changes to the proposal section is robust given a change in research design necessitated by the data structure. These changes are also referenced in the appropriate sections of Chapter 5.

Important Changes and Updates to Information in Chapters 1-3

Chapters 1-3 detailed the formulation, relevant literature, and all methodological processes for the study. Between planning and execution, there are some notable changes. First, the original study proposal reported that data sets with missing values would be assessed on a case-by-case basis. However, the SurveyMonkey questionnaire was set up so that every question required a value. The participants could select "prefer not to answer" for the optional demographic questions, but a value was required for each question. Therefore, the only data sets with missing values belonged to participants who did not complete the survey. Since the informed consent stated that data would not be used if a participant chose to exit the survey before completion, all incomplete responses were discarded.

The most significant changes occurred as a result of the data structure. During assumptions testing, the scatterplots demonstrated violations of both linearity and monotonicity. Additionally, the outliers and normality of residuals assumptions were also violated in many of the variables and variable pairs. The significant violations to several assumptions necessitated changes to data analysis causing associated changes to preserve alignment. Linear regression was the data analysis procedure identified in the proposal; however, linear regression analysis requires that the data conform to a linear relationship, demonstrate normality of residuals, and have no significant outliers (Laerd Statistics, 2018c). The non-parametric alternative identified in the proposal, the Seigel estimator, requires monotonicity which was also violated. These assumptions, detailed extensively in the assumptions testing section, were significantly violated thereby necessitating a new data analysis approach.

Given the data structure, the study design changed from predictive correlation to associative correlation. This change in study design required several other elements of the study to be reframed to ensure proper alignment (see Table 4.1). Further references to all items in the alignment table will reflect these updated items rather than those identified and discussed in Chapters 1-3.

Table 4.1

Updated Alignment Table

Alignment Item	Alignment Item Description
Problem Space Need:	Conflict is implicated as a key predictor of relationship success or failure (Delatorre & Wagner, 2019). There are many points of convergence to suggest that mindfulness and romantic partner conflict behavior operate using shared mechanisms such as stress, emotion regulation, and non-judgement.
Problem Statement:	It was not known if and to what extent a correlation exists between the five mechanisms of mindfulness identified in the Five Facet Mindfulness Questionnaire and the six conflict strategy subdomains identified in the Romantic Partner Conflict Scale used by adults in a committed romantic relationship.
Purpose of the Study:	The purpose of this quantitative associative correlational study was to determine if and to what extent a correlation exists between the five mechanisms of mindfulness identified in the Five Facet Mindfulness Questionnaire and the six conflict strategy subdomains identified in the Romantic Partner Conflict Scale used by adults in a committed romantic relationship living in the mid-Atlantic region of the United States.
Variables:	Traits of mindfulness (identified as acting with awareness, observing, describing, non-reactivity, and non-judging by the FFMQ) measured at the individual level; Romantic partner conflict strategy subdomains (identified as compromising, domination, submission, avoidance, separation, and interactional reactivity by the RPCS) measured at the individual level.
Research Questions:	RQ1: If and to what extent does a statistically significant correlation exist between acting with awareness and the conflict strategy subdomains used between adults in a committed romantic relationship?
	RQ2: If and to what extent does a statistically significant correlation exist between observing and the conflict strategy subdomains used between adults in a committed romantic relationship?
	RQ3: If and to what extent does a statistically significant correlation exist between describing and the conflict strategy subdomains used between adults in a committed romantic relationship?
	RQ4: If and to what extent does a statistically significant correlation exist between non-judging and the conflict strategy subdomains used between adults in a committed romantic relationship?
	RQ5: If and to what extent does a statistically significant correlation exist between non-reactivity and the conflict strategy subdomains used between adults in a committed romantic relationship?
Methodology/Research Design:	Quantitative Associative Correlational

As discussed in the proposal, a predictive correlational design requires the determination of a linear relationship. Previous studies reported the use of multiple linear regression implying that the data collected in those studies satisfied the assumption of linearity (see Harvey et al., 2015; Harvey et al., 2019). The violation of the linearity assumption in this study represents a significant departure from the existing research in this area. This is discussed further in sections of Chapter 5.

Preparation of Raw Data for Analysis and Tests of Assumptions

Preparation of Raw Data for Analysis

The raw data was exported from SurveyMonkey in an .SAV to be opened and cleaned directly in SPSS. First the 23 incomplete data sets were removed per the informed consent which stated that the information collected prior to a participant's decision to exit the survey would not be used in the study. Next, the researcher checked the data set for duplicates, and none were found. As SurveyMonkey was programmed to require the respondent to select an answer for each question, there was no missing data in the data set. There were also no erroneous responses as respondents were not permitted to select options outside of the valid survey responses. There were no data entry errors to correct as the data was imported directly to SPSS from SurveyMonkey. One demographic answer was altered. The participant selected 2 options under race (Asian and White), so the response was changed to 'other.' There were several outliers in the data set which contributed to the need to change the data analysis procedure as discussed previously. Outliers are defined as values which are two or more standard deviations away from the mean (Kwak & Kim, 2017). These outliers (see Table 4.2) were left in the data set as they represent valid responses and do not prevent accurate data analysis using Kendall's Tau-b. Unlike linear regression analysis, Kendall's Tau-b does not require the assumption that there are no significant outliers in the data set.

The demographic responses exported from SurveyMonkey required some preparation as the questions were divided by response and each response was listed as '1.00' under the column for that response choice. First, the responses under each column were changed to correspond with the answer choice. Then the columns for each question were merged so that each demographic question consisted of one column with values matching the respondents' answer. To illustrate this, the first demographic question related to age. When exported from SurveyMonkey there were seven columns for the age question. Each box was either blank or marked '1.00' if the respondent selected that answer choice. The first column was left as '1.00', the second was changed to '2.00', and so forth. Thus, when all seven columns were merged, there was one column representing the age demographic question and the numbers represented the respondent's age selection.

To begin scoring the research instruments, the reverse scored items from the FFMQ were transformed to reflect scoring for analysis. Next, the subscales scores were calculated in SPSS by using the Scale and Mean functions. The 7 demographic items, 5 subscales from the FFMQ, and 6 subscales from the RPCS were transferred to a new SPSS data sheet and labeled "cleaned data ready for analysis." The exported data set showed 126 responses; however, 23 incomplete sets were removed per the informed consent statement that information collected prior to a participant's decision to exit the survey would not be used in the study. The final data set was comprised of 103 responses.

The minimum required number of responses based on the G*Power a priori analysis was 85. After adding an additional 13 participants (15%) for violation of parametric assumptions, the minimum required sample size for the study was 98 participants. The final data set contained $N = 103$ for statistical analysis.

Tests of Assumptions

Assumption testing began with the assumptions for the linear regression analysis as identified in the proposal. The assumptions are continuous predictor and criterion variables, linearity, no significant outliers, independent observations, homoscedasticity, and normality of residuals. Most assumptions are tested using graphical or statistical measures and all are assessed as either satisfying or failing to satisfy the assumption.

Assumption 1 and 2: Continuous Variables. The first two assumptions were met prior to data collection. These assumptions require criterion and predictor variables measured on a continuous scale. These assumptions were satisfied based on the recommendation in Boone and Boone (2012) that Likert-scale data could be treated as continuous for the purpose of statistical analysis.

Assumption 3: Linearity. Each of the five research questions poses a set of six regressions, and the scatterplots for each are laid out in the following series of figures. A Loess line is included with each of the graphs to demonstrate the degree of linearity. A Loess line is a type of fit line which integrates parametric and non-parametric analysis to demonstrate the degree of linearity in a scatterplot when data trends may be hard to visually assess (USEPA, 2016). Each figure is accompanied by a narrative evaluating the presence of absence of a linear relationship for each of the featured scatterplots.

Figure 1

Scatterplots for Research Question One

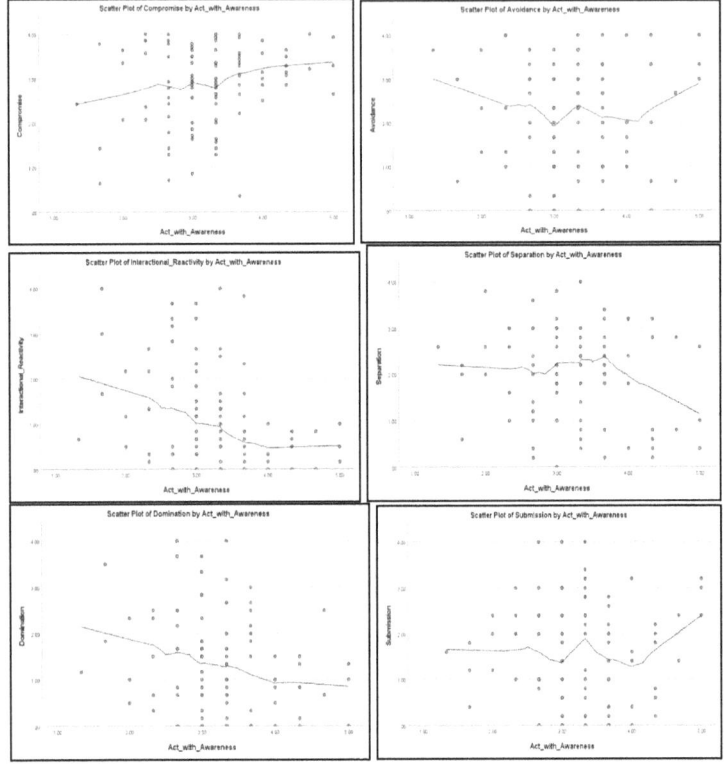

The scatterplots for acting with awareness/compromise, acting with awareness/interactional reactivity, and acting with awareness/domination appear to satisfy the linearity assumption. There is not a clear violation of linearity between acting with awareness/avoidance, acting with awareness/separation, and acting with awareness/domination. The violation is most clearly represented by the acting with awareness/avoidance graph, which appears U shaped. Graphically, those in the left column satisfy the linearity assumption, while those in the right column violate the assumption.

Figure 2

Scatterplots for Research Question Two

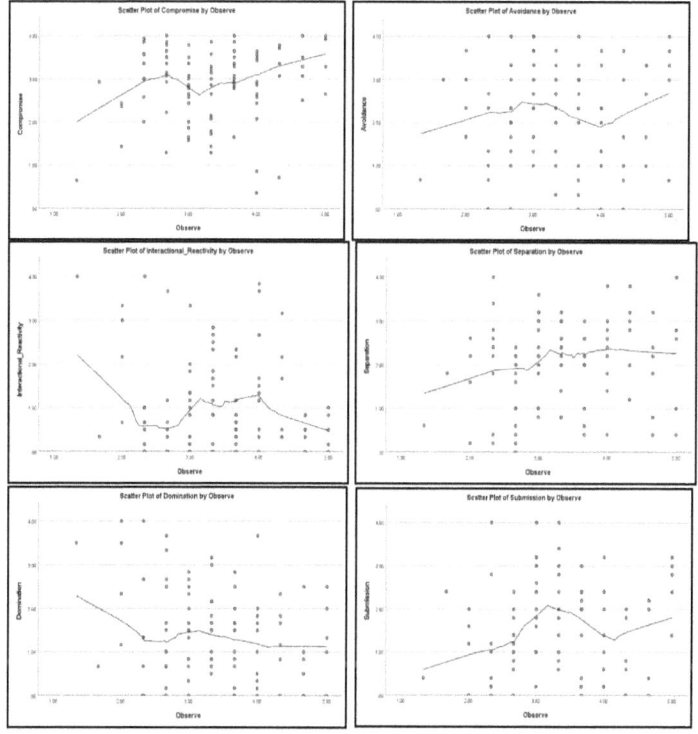

The scatterplots demonstrating a linear relationship between observe and a conflict strategy subdomain are compromise, separation, and domination. The conflict strategy subdomains which violate the assumption of linearity with the observe facet of mindfulness are avoidance, interactional reactivity, and submission. These subdomains demonstrate a significant peak or valley which preclude the validity of a linear model for analysis.

Figure 3

Scatterplots for Research Question Three

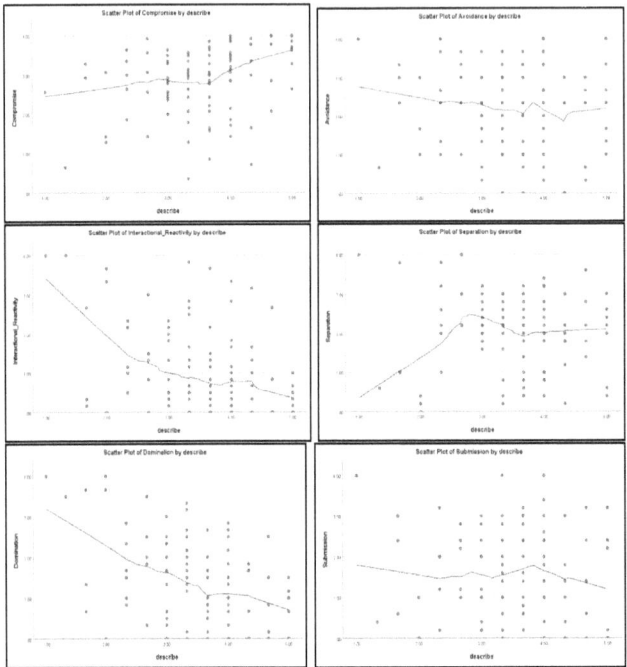

The conflict strategy subdomains which satisfy the assumption of linearity with the describing facet of mindfulness are compromise, avoidance, domination, and submission. The violating subdomains are interactional reactivity and separation (middle row). A clear violation is the separation scatterplot which begin very linear before plateauing near the mid-section of the data set. The interactional reactivity and describing variable pair appear to have an exponential rather than linear graphical relationship.

Figure 4

Scatterplots for Research Question Four

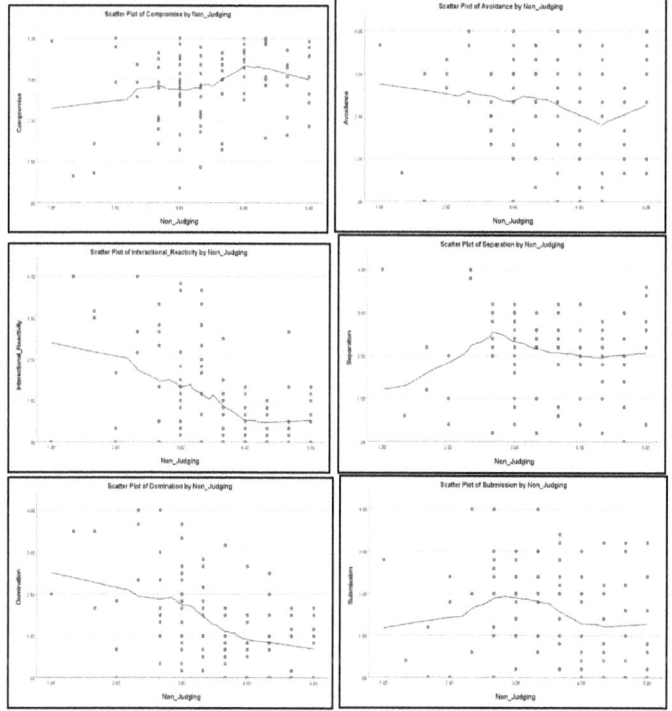

All subdomains except separation are inconclusive and could be considered linear enough to satisfy the assumption and continue with assumptions testing and parametric analysis provided that the other assumptions are met. The separation subdomain begins linear then demonstrates a wide U-shaped slope in the opposite direction. This is a violation of the linearity assumption.

Figure 5

Scatterplots for Research Question Five

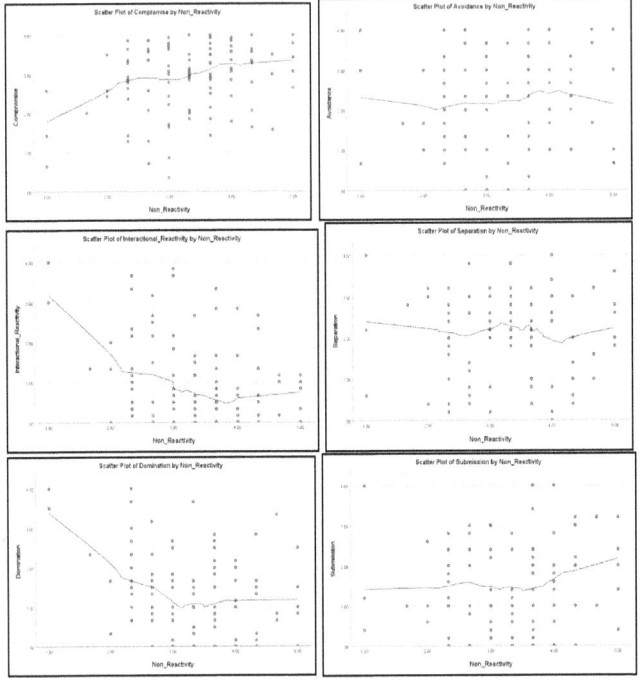

The conflict strategy subdomains that satisfy the linearity assumption when paired with the non-reactivity facet of mindfulness are compromise, avoidance, separation, and submission. While none are textbook linear graphical representation, they do appear linear enough to justify parametric testing. The interactional reactivity and domination subdomains violate the linearity assumption, and both are represented by steep downward slopes followed by a plateau.

These scatterplots demonstrate that the assumption of linearity for the linear regression analysis proposed in Chapter 3 was violated for approximately half of the variable pairs. The scatterplots also demonstrate that some variable pairings display monotonicity (e.g., acting with awareness/interactional reactivity, non-reactivity/domination, and describing/compromise) while others violate even the monotonicity assumption. Again, the assumption of monotonicity is required for many non-parametric tests including the Siegel Estimator which was the planned alternative.

Assumption 4: Outliers. The fourth assumption which must be satisfied for parametric linear regression analysis is the absence of outliers which significantly affect the strength and direction of the regression line. Highlighted in Table 4.2, it is clear that while some variables satisfy this assumption, other variables demonstrate a significant violation. Non-parametric tests are less sensitive to the impact of outliers and are therefore preferred given the presence of multiple or significant outliers (Mishra et al., 2019). The study procedures precluded the possibility for erroneous outliers; therefore, all outliers in the data set represent valid participant responses and to remove valid responses would reduce the validity and reliability of the study results.

Table 4.2

Outliers by Variable

Variable	Number of outliers in the data set
Mindfulness:	
Acting with Awareness	9
Observing	0
Describing	2
Non-judging	1
Non-reactivity	0
Conflict Strategies	
Compromise	3
Avoidance	0
Interactional Reactivity	5
Domination	0
Submission	0
Separation	0
Total:	20

Assumption 5: Independent Observations. The fifth required assumption to ensure the appropriateness of a parametric analysis is to verify independent observations. As discussed in chapter 3, this is achieved by using the Durbin-Watson test for autocorrelation. To satisfy this assumption, the Durbin-Watson statistic should be between 1.5 and 2.5 out of a possible range of 0 to 4 (Turner et al., 2021). Table 4.3 lists the correlation of residuals using the Durbin-Watson statistic. All variable pairings are within the acceptable range. The assumption of independent observations is satisfied.

Table 4.3

Durbin-Watson Statistics

	Compromise	Avoidance	Interactional Reactivity	Separation	Domination	Submission
Acting with Awareness	2.04	1.97	2.12	2.17	2.12	1.95
Observing	2.11	1.98	2.07	2.14	2.11	1.97
Describing	2.12	1.96	2.04	2.12	2.06	1.93
Non-judging	1.97	1.99	1.93	2.14	2.13	1.95
Non-reactivity	2.09	1.98	2.13	2.12	2.24	1.96

Assumption 6: Homoscedasticity. Homoscedasticity is graphically demonstrated using the same scatterplots as assumption 3 (see Figures 1-5). Homoscedasticity is evidenced through even spread of data versus fanned or funneled (Laerd Statistics, 2018c). The vast majority of the scatterplots demonstrate even spread, with an exception being the non-judging/domination scatterplot; however, Ernst and Albers (2017) endorse the use of a parametric linear regression analysis even when the homoscedasticity assumption is violated.

Assumption 7: Normality of Residuals. Normality of residuals can be graphically demonstrated using a histogram with a normality curve or a P-P plot. Per the proposed procedures in chapter 3, the normality of the residuals for this study will be graphically represented using a P-P plot. To satisfy this assumption, all data points should be close to the regression of standardized residuals line. This assumption is violated when the data points stray significantly from the line. Figures 6-10 organize the P-P plots by research question, just as was done with the scatterplots under assumption 3.

Figure 6

P-P plots for RQ1 – Acting with Awareness

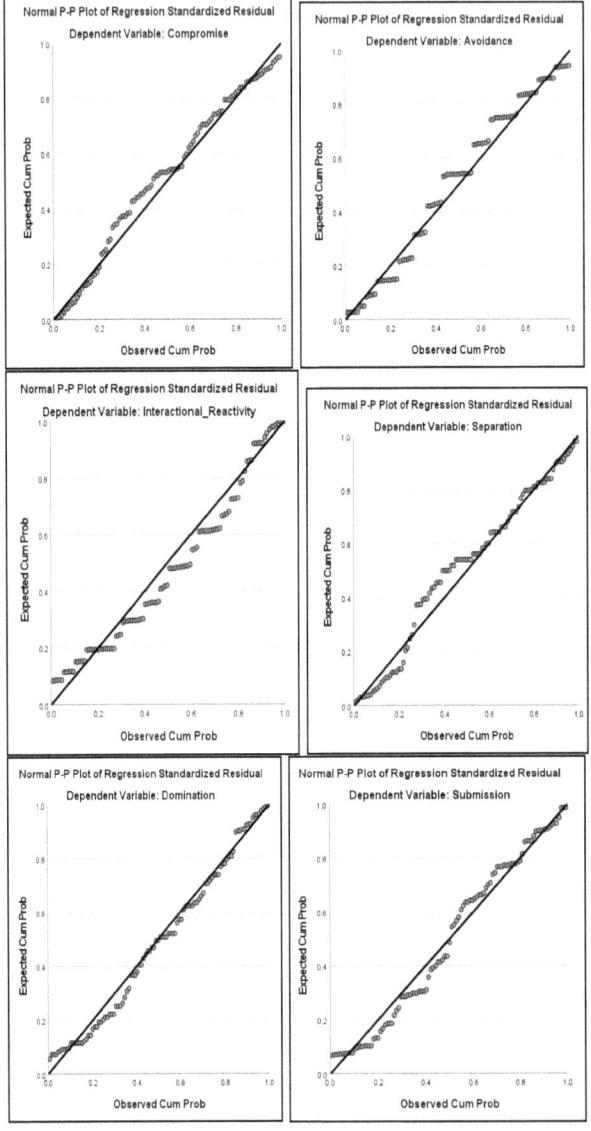

Figure 6 demonstrates that in each of the P-P plots there are areas with questionable normality. None of the graphs have outstanding deviations away from the regression line. The normality of residuals assumption is satisfied for RQ1.

Figure 7

P-P plots for RQ2 - Observing

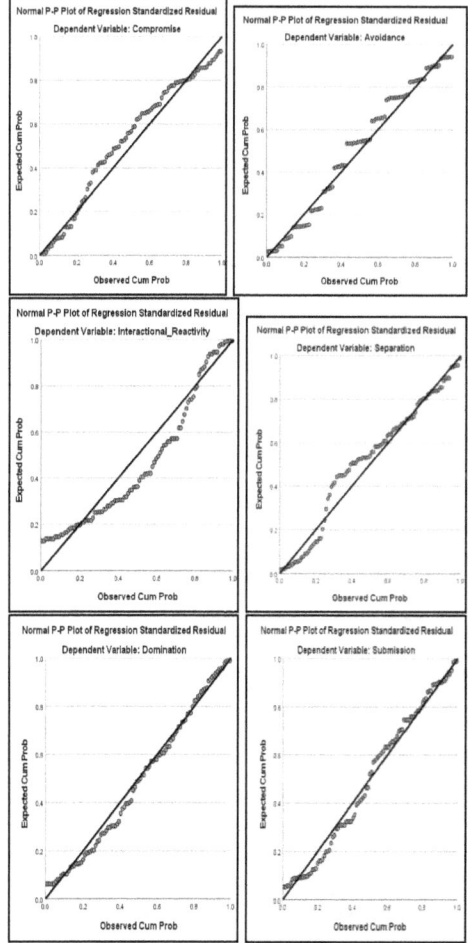

The P-P plots demonstrate more significant deviations for RQ2 than those from RQ1 (Figure 6). The results from this assumptions test are mixed. Primarily the interactional reactivity and separation subdomains of romantic partner conflict strategy demonstrate a violation of the normality of residuals assumption.

Figure 8

P-P plots for RQ3 - Describing

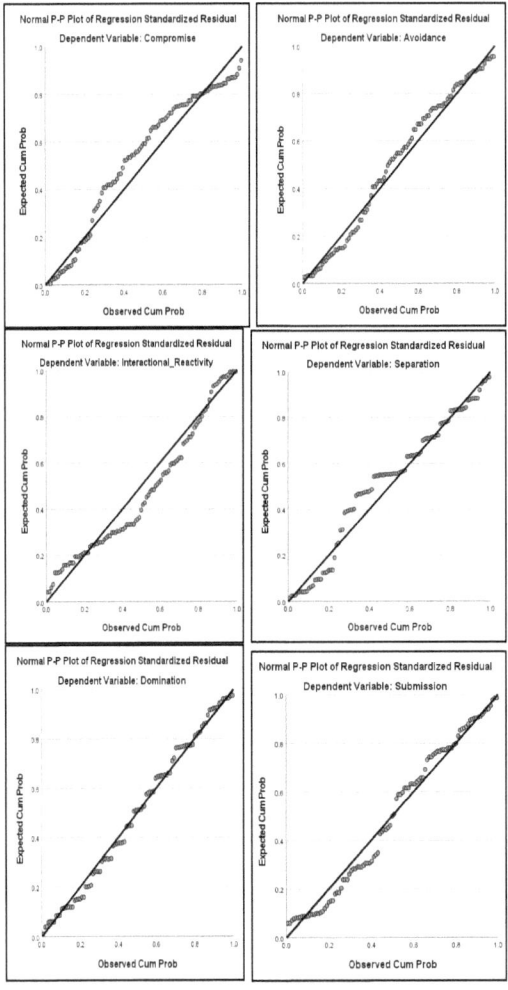

The results from the P-P plots for RQ3 are mixed. The avoidance, domination, and submission P-P plots satisfy the normality assumption; however, the compromise, interactional reactivity, and separation subdomains of conflict strategy represent violations to the normality of residuals assumption.

Figure 9

P-P plots for RQ4 – Non-judging

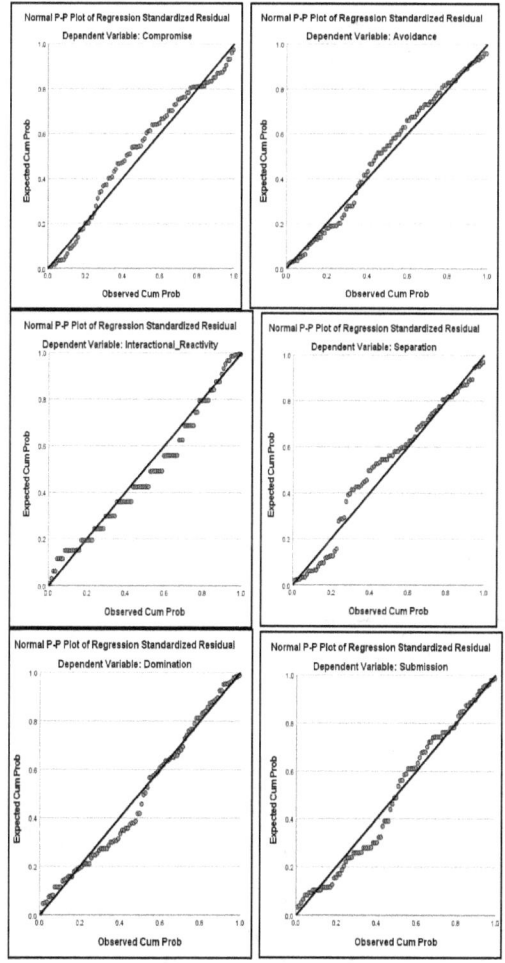

The P-P plots for RQ4 present with mixed results. The submission subdomain of conflict strategies has a bimodal rather than normal distribution. The domination, separation, and compromise subdomains also demonstrate some variation from normal. The normality of residuals assumption is violated for RQ4.

Figure 10

P-P plots for RQ5 – Non-reactivity

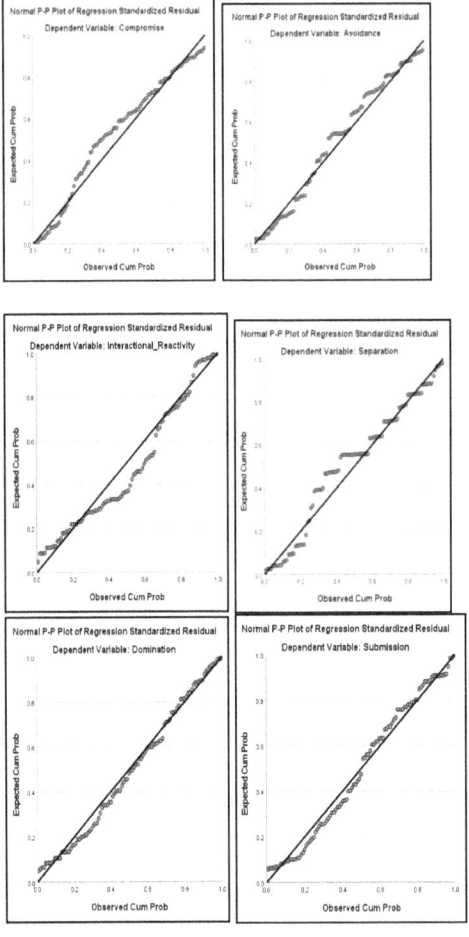

Compromise, interactional reactivity, and separation subdomains have significant deviations away from the regression line representing non-normality. The domination, submission, and avoidance subdomains are clustered tightly to the regression line which represents normality of residuals. This represents mixed results wherein some of the variable pairing satisfy the assumption while others violate.

Assessing the Results of Assumptions Testing. Many of the assumptions tests yielded mixed results; therefore, a detailed assessment and holistic interpretation is required. Mishra et al. (2019) warns against continuing with parametric analysis when the assumptions are in question as it hinders the interpretation and devalues the conclusions of the study. The researchers note that it is tempting for researchers to ignore assumptions violations so that the research can proceed with a parametric test with more statistical power; however, the consequence is the potential for invalid conclusions which appear statistically significant (Dwivedi & Shukla, 2020). For this reason, all violations of assumptions must be treated as significant unless otherwise noted in the literature (e.g., the homoscedasticity assumption). Similarly, the primary factor determining the data analysis method should be the alignment between study design, data structure, and data analysis (Mishra et al., 2019); therefore, the data analysis method should reflect the best match to the data even if that requires a change from parametric to nonparametric analysis.

The first two assumptions for parametric linear regression analysis were satisfied per the recommendation in Boone and Boone (2012) to treat Likert-scale data as continuous for the purpose of data analysis. However, assumption three was frequently violated as there is no graphically discernable linear relationship between many of the predictor and criterion variables (see Figures 1-5). Assumption 4, no significant outliers, was also violated by several of the predictor and criterion variables (see Table 4.2). Assumption 5, independent observations, was satisfied for all variable pairings per the

Durbin-Watson statistics reported in Table 4.3. Assumption 6, homoscedasticity, was primarily satisfied and there is an endorsement in the literature to proceed with parametric testing even when this assumption is violated (see Ernst & Albers, 2017). Assumption 7, normality of residuals, was tested using a P-P plot and this assumption was also frequently violated.

Correct analysis based on study design and data structure is crucial to ensure validity and reliability of the study findings and conclusions. While there is evidence to support that some of the data meets the assumptions for parametric linear regression analysis, there are several significant violations. These violations primarily occur for the linearity, outliers, and normality of residuals assumptions. Laerd Statistics (2018c) and Shreffler and Huecker (2023) recommend the use of nonparametric tests given these types of assumptions violations. The decision to use a nonparametric test for all research questions and hypotheses is based on two important factors. First, conducting parametric linear regression given the assumptions violations reduces the validity and reliability of the study. Second, all hypotheses should be tested using the same method of statistical analysis to allow for comparison and interpretation of the overall results of the study; therefore, the best choice for statistical analysis is the one which can be applied to all hypotheses in the study with no assumptions violations.

The non-parametric alternative identified in the proposal was the Siegel estimator; however, the lack of monotonicity combined with the necessity of an established linear relationship prior to conducting predictive analysis led to the determination that a non-parametric associative correlation was a more appropriate choice. The data structure precludes the use of linear regression analysis as well as non-parametric analyses that require the assumption of a monotonic relationship. A monotonic relationship is one in which the data points tend in a given direction but not as uniformly or directly as in a linear relationship (Laerd Statistics, 2018e). Therefore, all linear relationships are monotonic, but not all monotonic relationships are linear. For many of the variable pairing, the data structure demonstrates a violation of not only a linear relationship, but also a monotonic relationship. This requires the use of a statistical procedure that does not have the assumption of linearity or monotonicity. Laerd Statistics (2018e) recommends Kendall's Tau-b as an alternative to the more commonly used Spearman's rho and Siegel estimator when there is a violation of monotonicity. The change from linear regression to Kendall's tau-b is significant and is discussed in the appropriate sections of chapters 4 and 5.

Following the determination of neither linearity nor monotonicity, the assumption testing for Kendall's tau-b began. There are two assumptions for Kendall's Tau-b as identified by Laerd Statistics (2018b). The assumptions are related to variables and monotonicity. The first assumption is that the two variables used for analysis should be measured on an ordinal or continuous scale (Laerd Statistics, 2018b). This assumption was satisfied prior to data collection because all variables were measured using Likert-scale data which is ordinal. The second assumption is that there is a monotonic relationship between the variables; however, unlike other tests which require this assumption to be satisfied, Kendall's tau-b is still an appropriate test when the data do not appear monotonic (Laerd Statistics, 2018b). The next section details the descriptive findings from both the demographic and research data.

Descriptive Findings

The target population for this study was adults in a committed romantic relationship living in the mid-Atlantic region of the US. A convenience sample using a flyer on approved sites with a SurveyMonkey link yielded 103 completed and usable responses. The demographic questions related to age and state of residence were required because they are inclusion criteria. While participants were offered a "prefer not to answer" answer choice for the optional demographics (gender, race, education, length of relationship, and formal mindfulness training) this option was selected only by 3 participants for the race demographic question. The following section details the demographic statistics of the participants who make up the sample for this study.

Demographic Statistics

The majority of the participants were female (82%), white (85%), and had minimal or no formal mindfulness training (73%). Regarding age, the most frequent age selection was 26-35 (38.8%). There was at least 1 participant in each age range (see Table 4.4).

Table 4.4

Demographic Statistics – Age

Participant Age	Frequency	Percent (%)
18-25	14	13.6
26-35	40	38.8
36-45	21	20.4
46-55	12	11.7
56-65	10	9.7
66-75	3	2.9
76-85	2	1.9
86-95	1	1.0
Total	103	100.0

While the sample includes respondents from each of the five included states, 68% of the respondents reported Maryland as their state of residence (see Table 4.5). This uneven representation is discussed in the limitations section of Chapter 5. Stratified random sampling could have been used to ensure an equal number of participants from each state.

Table 4.5

Demographic Statistics – State of Residence

Participant State of Residence	Frequency	Percent (%)
Delaware	2	1.9
Maryland	70	68.0
Pennsylvania	17	16.5
Virginia	7	6.8
West Virginia	7	6.8
Total	103	100

The following demographic statistics were optional, so the questionnaire included a "prefer not to answer" answer selection. All questions required a response, so respondents were required to either select a demographic option or select the "prefer not to answer" option. Therefore, despite being optional, all demographic statistics contain $N = 103$. Gender was the first optional demographic participants encountered. Although there were 7 options available, participants only used the "female" and "male" gender options. Table 4.6 describes the gender profile of the sample.

Table 4.6

Demographic Statistics – Gender

Participant Gender	Frequency	Percent (%)
Female	84	81.6
Male	19	18.4
Non-Binary	0	0
Transgender Female	0	0
Transgender Male	0	0
Prefer not to answer	0	0
Other	0	0
Total	103	100

The next optional demographic was race. The SurveyMonkey questionnaire allowed participants to select more than one option, so the one participant who selected both "Asian" and "White" was changed to "Other." There was a "Native American or American Indian" option, but no participants selected it. The racial demographics are summarized in Table 4.7.

Table 4.7

Demographic Statistics – Race

Participant Race	Frequency	Percent (%)
Asian or Pacific Islander	2	1.9
Black or African American	7	6.8
Hispanic or Latino	2	1.9
Native American or American Indian	0	0
White or Caucasian	88	85.4
Prefer not to answer	3	2.0
Other	1	1.0
Total	103	100

Participants were asked to select the length of their relationship from various groupings. Prior research by Harvey et al. (2015) discussed length of the relationship as a significant factor influencing conflict strategy use. Table 4.8 provides an overview of the sample distribution related to relationship length.

Table 4.8

Demographic Statistics – Length of Relationship

Relationship Length	Frequency	Percent (%)
Less than 1 year	7	6.8
Between 1 and 5 years	28	27.2
Between 5 and 15 years	37	35.9
Between 15 and 25 years	11	10.7
More than 25 years	20	19.4
Prefer not to answer	0	0
Total	103	100

Prior research also implicates education as a significant factor influencing romantic relationship interactions. The study sample represents a sample of considerably higher education than the general population (see Table 4.9). Additionally, several participants selected more than one education option (for example, both bachelor's degree and master's degree). In such cases, the participant's highest level of education is represented.

Table 4.9

Demographic Statistics – Education

Highest Level of Education	Frequency	Percent (%)
Nursery school to 8th grade	0	0
Some high school, no diploma	1	1.0
High school graduation; diploma or equivalent (E.g., GED)	5	5.8
Some college credit, no degree	23	22.3
Trade/Technical/Vocational	2	1.9
Associate Degree	8	7.8
Bachelor's Degree	28	27.2
Master's Degree	28	27.2
Professional Degree	3	2.9
Doctorate Degree	5	4.9
Prefer not to answer	0	0
Total	103	100

The final demographic question asked participants to indicate their level of formal mindfulness training. Formal mindfulness training was defined for participants as yoga, meditation, or tai chi classes or training. Literature on mindfulness suggests that mindfulness training does improve mindfulness scores on instruments; however, even people with no formal mindfulness experience may still have high scores on a mindfulness measure. This can be explained by the integration of mindfulness skills and philosophy into programs, religions, and treatments without being explicitly taught as or even called mindfulness. The study sample is composed primarily of individuals who reported their formal mindfulness training as none or minimal (see Table 4.10).

Table 4.10

Demographic Statistics – Formal Mindfulness Training

Training Rate	Frequency	Percent (%)
None	40	38.8
Minimal (less than 10 classes / lifetime)	35	34.0
Moderate (10-30 classes/lifetime OR less than 6/year)	13	12.6
Frequent (more than 6 classes/year)	4	3.9
Monthly	2	1.9
Weekly	4	3.9
Daily	5	4.9
Prefer not to answer	0	0
Total	103	100

Table 4.11 summarizes the descriptive statistics for the research variables. The mechanisms of mindfulness were measured using the FFMQ-15. The conflict strategy subdomains were measured using the RPCS.

Table 4.11

Research Variables – Descriptive Statistics

Variable	Min	Max	M(SD)	Skewness	Kurtosis
Mechanisms of Mindfulness					
Observe	1.33	5.00	3.36 (.82)	.10	-.51
Describe	1.00	5.00	3.50 (.87)	-.43	.12
Act with Awareness	1.33	5.00	3.24 (.72)	.08	.53
Non-Judging	1.00	5.00	3.53 (.90)	-.24	-.22
Non-Reactivity	1.00	5.00	3.32 (.87)	-.30	.17
Conflict Strategy Subdomains					
Compromise	.36	4.00	2.88 (.85)	-.89	.24
Avoidance	.00	4.00	2.21 (1.15)	-.28	-.92
Interactional Reactivity	.00	4.00	1.09 (1.08)	1.13	.39
Separation	.00	4.00	2.07 (.96)	-.36	-.51
Domination	.00	4.00	1.38 (1.05)	.54	-.36
Submission	.00	4.00	1.59 (1.09)	.18	-.95

Reliability. The Cronbach's alpha (α) is the standard measurement for internal reliability. Table 4.12 demonstrates that only one scale fell short of the minimum reliability score of α = .7. All other variables demonstrate acceptable levels of internal reliability.

Table 4.12

Reliability Statistics – Cronbach's Alpha

Scale	α
Mechanisms of Mindfulness	
Observe	.61
Describe	.84
Act with Awareness	.70
Non-Judging	.84
Non-Reactivity	.78
Conflict Strategy Subdomains	
Compromise	.95
Interactional Reactivity	.90
Domination	.91
Submission	.94
Avoidance	.87
Separation	.86

The reliability of the observing scale of the FFMQ-15 is below the threshold of α = .7 which is also a deviation from previous reliability published during other studies that used the questionnaire. Due to the lack of reliable data, the observing facet of mindfulness will not be included for data analysis. The consequence is that RQ2 will not be answered, and the associated hypotheses will not be tested. This is discussed as a limitation at the end of Chapter 4 and again in related sections of Chapter 5. The remaining four facets of mindfulness from the FFMQ-15 have acceptable reliability levels and echo the findings of similar research. The reliability of the scales in the RPCS are all within the acceptable range and are very similar to those published in other studies.

The purpose of this quantitative associative correlational study was to determine if and to what extent a correlation exists between the five mechanisms of mindfulness identified in the Five Facet Mindfulness Questionnaire and the six conflict strategy subdomains identified in the Romantic Partner Conflict Scale used by adults in a committed romantic relationship living in the mid-Atlantic region of the United States. The following four research questions and associated hypotheses serve as the foundation of this study. As previously discussed, RQ2 is omitted due to the poor reliability of the observing facet of mindfulness.

RQ1: If and to what extent does a statistically significant correlation exist between acting with awareness and the conflict strategy subdomains used between adults in a committed romantic relationship?

H_o1: There is not a statistically significant correlation between acting with awareness and conflict strategy use between adults in a committed romantic relationship for the following subdomains:
- Compromise
- Avoidance
- Interactional Reactivity
- Separation
- Domination
- Submission

H$_a$1: There is a statistically significant correlation between acting with awareness and conflict strategy use between adults in a committed romantic relationship for the following subdomains:
- Compromise
- Avoidance
- Interactional Reactivity
- Separation
- Domination
- Submission

RQ3: If and to what extent does a statistically significant correlation exist between describing and the conflict strategy subdomains used between adults in a committed romantic relationship?

H$_o$3: There is not a statistically significant correlation between describing and conflict strategy use between adults in a committed romantic relationship for the following subdomains:
- Compromise
- Avoidance
- Interactional Reactivity
- Separation
- Domination
- Submission

H_a3: There is a statistically significant correlation between describing and conflict strategy use between adults in a committed romantic relationship for the following subdomains:
- Compromise
- Avoidance
- Interactional Reactivity
- Separation
- Domination
- Submission

RQ4: If and to what extent does a statistically significant correlation exist between non-judging and the conflict strategy subdomains used between adults in a committed romantic relationship?

H_o4: There is not a statistically significant correlation between non-judging and conflict strategy use between adults in a committed romantic relationship for the following subdomains:
- Compromise
- Avoidance
- Interactional Reactivity
- Separation
- Domination
- Submission

H_a4: There is a statistically significant correlation between non-judging and conflict strategy use between adults in a committed romantic relationship for the following subdomains:
- Compromise
- Avoidance
- Interactional Reactivity
- Separation
- Domination
- Submission

RQ5: If and to what extent does a statistically significant correlation exist between non-reactivity and the conflict strategy subdomains used between adults in a committed romantic relationship?

H_o5: There is not a statistically significant correlation between non-reactivity and conflict strategy use between adults in a committed romantic relationship for the following subdomains:
- Compromise
- Avoidance
- Interactional Reactivity
- Separation
- Domination
- Submission

H_a5: There is a statistically significant correlation between non-reactivity and conflict strategy use between adults in a committed romantic relationship for the following subdomains:

- Compromise
- Avoidance
- Interactional Reactivity
- Separation
- Domination
- Submission

Kendall's Tau-b was used to answer RQ1, and RQs 3-5. To answer each research question, six correlation analyses were conducted. Research Question 1 asks, if and to what extent does a statistically significant correlation exist between acting with awareness and the conflict strategy subdomains used between adults in a committed romantic relationship? The null hypothesis (to be rejected) is that the conflict strategy subdomains do not have a statistically significant correlation with acting with awareness. The alternative hypothesis states that the conflict strategy subdomains have a statistically significant correlation with acting with awareness. RQ1 requires six hypothesis tests, and each will either reject or fail to reject the null hypothesis for the given conflict strategy subdomain. These hypotheses were tested using SPSS, bivariate correlate, Kendall's Tau-b (2-tailed). The SPSS output is the correlation table with the correlation coefficient and significance along with the N. The N, total sample size, was always 103 since there were 103 complete and valid data sets. The results of the data analysis are presented in Table 4.13

Table 4.13

Results of Data Analysis – Correlation Coefficient (Significance)

	Compromise	Avoidance	Interactional Reactivity	Separation	Domination	Submission
Acting with Awareness	.137 (.058)	-.015 (.841)	-.230 (.002)*	-.023 (.752)	-.195 (.007)*	.009 (.901)
Describing	.241 (<.001)*	-.045 (.536)	-.209 (.004)*	-.038 (.603)	-.264 (<.001)*	-.026 (.723)
Non-Judging	.156 (.028)	-.089 (.220)	-.274 (<.001)*	-.095 (.188)	-.350 (<.001)*	-.146 (.043)
Non-Reactivity	.185 (.009)	.059 (.414)	-.176 (.015)	-.020 (.777)	-.178 (.014)	.064 (.374)

* Significant at the 0.008 level

The answer to RQ1 requires six correlation analyses corresponding to the six hypotheses which correspond to the six conflict strategy subdomains. The six subdomains are compromise, avoidance, interactional reactivity, separation, domination, and submission. Therefore, six null hypotheses will either be rejected or fail to be rejected. For RQ1, the null hypothesis was rejected and there is a statistically significant correlation between acting with awareness and conflict strategy use between adults in a committed romantic relationship for the following subdomains: interactional reactivity and domination. There is also a failure to reject the null hypothesis, which states that there is not a statistically significant correlation between acting with awareness and conflict strategy use between adults in a committed romantic relationship, for the following subdomains: compromise, avoidance, separation, and submission. The results of the hypothesis testing answer the research question by determining if and to what extent there is a statistically significant correlation between acting with awareness and the six conflict strategy subdomains in the RPCS.

RQs 3-5 are answered in the same way, each with a different facet of mindfulness alongside the six conflict strategy subdomains; therefore, the maximum repetitions for the use of any one data set is six. This mirrors the proposal which included a Bonferroni correction to account for six repetitions in data use during analysis. As discussed in Chapter 3, a Bonferroni correction adjusts the required significance level to preserve validity despite repeated use of the same data (Lee & Lee, 2018). This study uses a significance level of .008 which is equivalent to .05 (the standard significance level) divided by six (the number of repeated uses of a single set of data). Therefore, a correlation coefficient must have a significance level of $p < .008$ in order for the correlation to be deemed as statistically significant.

Results

This section details the results of the correlation analyses as is used to answer the research questions. Correlation analysis is an examination of the presence and strength of the relationship between the mechanisms of mindfulness identified in the Five Facet Mindfulness Questionnaire (Baer et al., 2006) and the six conflict strategy subdomains identified in the Romantic Partner Conflict Scale (Zacchilli et al., 2009). The research questions were derived from the purpose of the study which was to determine if and to what extent a correlation exists between the five mechanisms of mindfulness identified in the FFMQ and the six conflict strategy subdomains identified in the RPCS as used by adults in a committed romantic relationship living in the mid-Atlantic region of the United States.

Presenting the Results

The results of Kendall's tau-b correlation analysis are judged by a significance level of $p < .008$. The significance level is the result of a Bonferroni correction to account for six repetitions of data use during analysis. Any result with significance above .008

will be deemed insignificant for this study. There are 24 hypotheses tested for this study as there are six for each of four research questions. Therefore, for each research question, the null hypothesis that there is no statistically significant correlation is assessed and either rejected or failed to be rejected for each of the six conflict strategy subdomains. To reject the null hypothesis, a conflict strategy subdomain must have a significant correlation with the facet of mindfulness at the $p < .008$ level.

Research Question One

RQ1: If and to what extent does a statistically significant correlation exist between acting with awareness and the conflict strategy subdomains used between adults in a committed romantic relationship?

H_o1: There is not a statistically significant correlation between acting with awareness and conflict strategy use between adults in a committed romantic relationship for the following subdomains:

- Compromise
- Avoidance
- Interactional Reactivity
- Separation
- Domination
- Submission

H_a1: There is a statistically significant correlation between acting with awareness and conflict strategy use between adults in a committed romantic relationship for the following subdomains:

- Compromise

- Avoidance
- Interactional Reactivity
- Separation
- Domination
- Submission

Results of Kendall's Tau-b for RQ1. A Kendall's Tau-b correlation analysis provided mixed results to answer the first research question. There were two moderately strong negative correlations between acting with awareness/interactional reactivity ($\tau_b(103) = -.230, p = .002$) and acting with awareness/domination ($\tau_b(103) = -.195, p = .007$). The null hypothesis was rejected for the interactional reactivity and domination conflict strategy subdomains. There is a statistically significant correlation between acting with awareness and conflict strategy use between adults in a committed romantic relationship for the interactional reactivity and domination subdomains. The results failed to reject the null hypothesis for the compromise, avoidance, separation, and submission subdomains. There is not a statistically significant correlation between acting with awareness and conflict strategy use between adults in a committed romantic relationship for the compromise, avoidance, separation, and submission subdomains. The complete results of this analysis are documented in Table 4.14.

Table 4.14

Correlation Output – RQ1[a]

	Correlation Coefficient	Significance	Correlation Strength[b]
Compromise	.137	.058	Weak
Avoidance	-.015	.841	Very Weak
Interactional Reactivity	-.230	.002*	Moderate
Separation	-.023	.752	Very Weak
Domination	-.195	.007*	Moderate
Submission	.009	.901	Very Weak

[a] as correlated with Acting with Awareness, [b] per guidelines in Botsch (2011) * significant at the .008 level

Research Question Two

RQ2: If and to what extent does a statistically significant correlation exist between observing and the conflict strategy subdomains used between adults in a committed romantic relationship?

H_o2: There is not a statistically significant correlation between observing and conflict strategy use between adults in a committed romantic relationship for the following subdomains:

- Compromise
- Avoidance
- Interactional Reactivity
- Separation
- Domination
- Submission

H_a2: There is a statistically significant correlation between observing and conflict strategy use between adults in a committed romantic relationship for the following subdomains:

- Compromise
- Avoidance
- Interactional Reactivity
- Separation
- Domination
- Submission

Due to the low Cronbach's alpha score ($\alpha=.61$), the data related to the observing mechanism of mindfulness is deemed unreliable. No data analysis was completed to answer RQ2. There is no evidence to reject or fail to reject the null hypotheses. The context and implications of this result are discussed in the relevant sections of Chapter 5.

Research Question Three

RQ3: If and to what extent does a statistically significant correlation exist between describing and the conflict strategy subdomains used between adults in a committed romantic relationship?

H_o3: There is not a statistically significant correlation between describing and conflict strategy use between adults in a committed romantic relationship for the following subdomains:

- Compromise
- Avoidance
- Interactional Reactivity
- Separation
- Domination
- Submission

H_a3: There is a statistically significant correlation between describing and conflict strategy use between adults in a committed romantic relationship for the following subdomains:

- Compromise
- Avoidance
- Interactional Reactivity
- Separation
- Domination
- Submission

Results of Kendall's Tau-b for RQ3. Just as for RQ1, this research question was answered through interpretation of the SPSS output of a Kendall's Tau-b correlation between the describing mechanism of mindfulness and the six conflict strategy subdomains identified in the RPCS. The results (see Table 4.15) indicate three moderately strong and significant correlations between describing/compromise ($\tau_b(103) = .241, p < .001$), describing/interactional reactivity ($\tau_b(103) = -.209, p = .004$), and describing/domination ($\tau_b(103) = -.264, p < .001$). Based on these results, the null hypothesis is rejected for the compromise, interactional reactivity, and domination subdomains. There is a failure to reject the null hypothesis for the avoidance, separation, and submission subdomains because there is not a statistically significant correlation between describing and use of avoidance, separation, and submission between adults in a committed romantic relationship per the results of this study.

Table 4.15

Correlation Output – RQ3[a]

	Correlation Coefficient	Significance	Correlation Strength[b]
Compromise	.241	<.001*	Moderate
Avoidance	-.045	.536	Very Weak
Interactional Reactivity	-.209	.004*	Moderate
Separation	-.038	.603	Very Weak
Domination	-.264	<.001*	Moderate
Submission	.026	.723	Very Weak

[a] as correlated with Describing, [b] per guidelines in Botsch (2011) * significant at the .008 level

Research Question Four

RQ4: If and to what extent does a statistically significant correlation exist between non-judging and the conflict strategy subdomains used between adults in a committed romantic relationship?

H_o4: There is not a statistically significant correlation between non-judging and conflict strategy use between adults in a committed romantic relationship for the following subdomains:

- Compromise
- Avoidance
- Interactional Reactivity
- Separation
- Domination
- Submission

H_a4: There is a statistically significant correlation between non-judging and conflict strategy use between adults in a committed romantic relationship for the following subdomains:

- Compromise
- Avoidance
- Interactional Reactivity
- Separation
- Domination
- Submission

Results of Kendall's Tau-b for RQ4. The fourth research question is answered through interpretation of the significance of the correlation coefficients produced as a result of the Kendall's Tau-b correlation analysis for the non-judging mechanism of mindfulness and the six conflict strategy subdomains from the RPCS (see Table 4.16). The statistically significant correlations were interactional reactivity ($\tau_b(103) = -.274$, $p < .001$) and domination ($\tau_b(103) = -.350$, $p < .001$). Based on these results, the null hypothesis is rejected for the interactional reactivity and domination subdomains. The results of this study fail to reject the null hypothesis for the compromise, avoidance, separation, and submission subdomains of romantic partner conflict strategy.

Table 4.16

Correlation Output – RQ4[a]

	Correlation Coefficient	Significance	Correlation Strength[b]
Compromise	.156	.028	Weak
Avoidance	-.089	.220	Very Weak
Interactional Reactivity	-.274	<.001*	Moderate
Separation	-.095	.188	Weak
Domination	-.350	<.001*	Strong
Submission	.146	.043	Weak

[a] as correlated with Non-judging, [b] per guidelines in Botsch (2011) * significant at the .008 level

Research Question Five

RQ5: If and to what extent does a statistically significant correlation exist between non-reactivity and the conflict strategy subdomains used between adults in a committed romantic relationship?

H_o5: There is not a statistically significant correlation between non-reactivity and conflict strategy use between adults in a committed romantic relationship for the following subdomains:

- Compromise
- Avoidance
- Interactional Reactivity
- Separation
- Domination
- Submission

H_a5: There is a statistically significant correlation between non-reactivity and conflict strategy use between adults in a committed romantic relationship for the following subdomains:

- Compromise
- Avoidance
- Interactional Reactivity
- Separation
- Domination
- Submission

Results of Kendall's Tau-b for RQ5. This research question examines the presence of a statistically significant correlation between the non-reactivity mechanism of mindfulness and the six conflict strategy subdomains from the RPCS. Table 4.17 details the correlation coefficients along with their significance and strength. The results failed to reject the null hypothesis for each of the conflict strategy subdomains as none of the correlations reached significance at the .008 level. Three correlations were significant at the $p < .05$ level which is the standard significance level in the absence of a Bonferroni correction. This is discussed further in the limitations section of Chapter 4 and the relevant sections of Chapter 5.

Table 4.17

Correlation Output – RQ5[a]

	Correlation Coefficient	Significance	Correlation Strength[b]
Compromise	.185	.009	Weak
Avoidance	.059	.414	Very Weak
Interactional Reactivity	-.176	.015	Weak
Separation	-.020	.777	Very Weak
Domination	-.178	.014	Weak
Submission	.064	.374	Very Weak

[a] as correlated with Non-reactivity, [b] per guidelines in Botsch (2011) * significant at the .008 level

Limitations

Limitations include all aspects of a research study which decrease its validity and reliability. While all research has limitations, it is crucial to openly disclose the study limitations to preserve quality and academic integrity. Additionally, limitations provide a foundation from which to make recommendations for future research. Some limitations can be anticipated at the outset of a research study while others present during and after data collection. For this study, the anticipated limitations were response bias, convenience sampling, impact of COVID-19. The anticipate limitations were discussed in greater detail in Chapter 1. These limitations were apparent given the study parameters; however, it is impossible to detect the extent to which these factors influenced the results of the study.

These limitations pose a risk to the internal and external validity of the study. Internal validity is threatened by the inability to verify the accurateness of a participant's response. Participants may intentionally or unintentionally respond to the questions in a way that does not accurately reflect their mindfulness levels or their use of conflict strategies. Using a combination of self-report data and researcher observations would address this limitation. External validity, as it relates to generalizability, is limited by the use of convenience sampling. The individuals accessed and recruited through the social media recruitment campaign may not be representative of the target population. The target population for this study is the adults in a committed romantic relationship living in the mid-Atlantic region of the United States who are members of the identified Facebook groups used for recruiting.

In addition to these limitations, some additional limitations surfaced during the recruitment, data collection, and data analysis phases. The study was closed once the required 98 complete responses were obtained which took seven days with a surplus of 5 responses. It is possible that many of the members of the target population did not see the recruitment flyer prior to the questionnaire being closed. A second limitation is a non-representative sample. The study sample was primarily White (85.4%), female (81.6%), and highly educated (35% had a master's, professional, or doctorate degree). According to the U.S. Census Bureau's 2019 statistics, only 13.1% of the US population holds a master's, professional, or doctorate degree (U.S. Census Bureau, 2019). This represents a significant difference between the population of interest and the sample, and therefore constitutes a limitation to the generalizability of the results.

Another major limitation which presented after data collection is the transition from a predictive to an associative correlation design. The absence of a linear or monotonic relationship, presence of multiple and significant outliers, and lack of normality in the residuals in many of the data sets precluded the use of a predictive analysis and left Kendall's Tau-b as the most appropriate choice (see chapter 4 for more detail). Kendall's Tau-b is both non-parametric and correlation rather than the parametric regression analysis which was proposed. As discussed in Chapter 3, parametric tests are preferred because they have greater statistical power. Greater statistical power refers to the ability and accuracy of a test to detect a significant result (Ali & Bhaskar, 2016). This is a serious limitation because using Kendall's Tau-b instead of a parametric test, although required due to the data structure, increases the potential that a statistically significant correlation will be reported as insignificant. Similarly, the transition from predictive to associative design again limits the utility of the results because this study cannot make recommendations based on predictive power. A predictive design allows conclusions that a given variable is responsible for a certain amount of variation in an outcome variable. An associative design merely demonstrates that the variables vary together at a given rate. The associative design is the precursor for a predictive design, so the inability to conduct a predictive analysis is a significant limitation both statistically and conceptually.

Summary

The purpose of this quantitative associative correlational study was to determine if and to what extent a correlation exists between the five mechanisms of mindfulness identified in the Five Facet Mindfulness Questionnaire and the six conflict strategy subdomains identified in the Romantic Partner Conflict Scale used by adults in a committed romantic relationship living in the mid-Atlantic region of the United States. Chapter 4 details the data preparation and analysis including changes to the proposal, data cleaning, assumptions testing, and the data analysis procedures. Organizers such as tables, graphs, and charts illustrate sample demographics, descriptive statistics for the research variables, and scale reliability. Finally, the results of the data analysis were used to test the research hypotheses and answer the research questions.

The researcher posted the recruitment flyer on the approved Facebook groups following all required approvals (Appendix C). Participants clicked on the link provided and were immediately directed to a welcome page followed by the IRB-approved informed consent (Appendix D). After agreeing to the informed consent, participants were directed to 7 demographic questions (2 required, 5 optional) followed by the 15 items from the FFMQ-15 and the 39 items from the RPCS. The informed consent indicated that a participant's incomplete data would not be used if they decided to discontinue the survey before completion, so 23 incomplete data sets were removed leaving $N = 103$ for data analysis. The minimum required sample size was 98 participants based on the a priori power analysis completed using G*Power (Appendix F).

Based on $N = 103$, assumptions testing was initiated for the assumptions listed in Chapter 3, several assumptions were violated including linearity/monotonicity, outliers, and normality of residuals. This precluded the use of all parametric measures and many non-parametric measures including the identified plan B from Chapter 3. The study design was changed to associative correlational and data analysis was completed using Kendall's tau-b because the monotonicity assumption is not a strict requirement (see Laerd Statistics, 2018b). Data analysis revealed a range of statistically significant and insignificant correlations. RQ2 was removed due to a lack of reliable data related to the observing facet of mindfulness from the FFMQ-15. RQ1, and RQs 3-5 examined the correlations between the four remaining facets of mindfulness of the FFMQ-15 and the six conflict strategy subdomains in the RPCS.

The null hypothesis was rejected for RQ1 for the domination and interactional reactivity subdomains of romantic partner conflict strategy. The conclusion to reject these null hypotheses was based on the significant negative correlation with acting with awareness. Acting with awareness and interactional reactivity demonstrated a statistically significant negative correlation of $\tau_b(103) = -.230, p = .002$, and acting with awareness and domination demonstrated a statistically significant negative correlation of $\tau_b(103) = -.195, p = .007$. The other conflict strategies (compromise, avoidance, separation, and submission) did not yield statistically significant correlations with acting with awareness; therefore, the results failed to reject the null hypothesis that there is not a statistically significant correlation between acting with awareness and compromise, avoidance, separation, and submission use between adults in a committed romantic relationship.

For RQ3, the null hypothesis was rejected for the compromise, interactional reactivity, and domination subdomains. This conclusion is based on the significant results between describing/compromise ($\tau_b(103) = .241, p < .001$), describing/interactional reactivity ($\tau_b(103) = -.209$, $p = .004$), and describing/domination ($\tau_b(103) = -.264$, $p < .001$). These correlation coefficients demonstrate moderate strength in addition to statistical significance. The null hypothesis was not rejected for the avoidance, separation, and submission subdomains due to the lack of statistical significance in the correlations.

The null hypothesis was also rejected for the interactional reactivity and domination subdomains in RQ4 based on the significant results between non-judging/interactional reactivity ($\tau_b(103) = -.274$, $p < .001$) and non-judging/domination ($\tau_b(103) = -.350$, $p < .001$). Non-judging and domination produced the only strong correlation of the study. All others were identified as moderate or below based on the guidelines in Botsch (2011). For RQ4, the null hypothesis was not rejected for the compromise, avoidance, separation, and submission subdomains. The results for RQ5 represent a failure to reject the null hypothesis for each of the six conflict strategy subdomains because none of the correlation analyses produced a statistically significant result at the .008 level. The variable pair with the closest result to significance was non-reactivity and compromise which yielded a result of $\tau_b(103) = .185$, $p = .009$.

There are study limitations related to the planning and execution of the study. Anticipated limitations included the use of self-report data and convenience sampling, primarily. These limitations pose a risk to the internal and external validity of the study because it is possible that the answers provided to the survey questions might not be accurate and cannot be verified, and that the sample will not be representative of the target population. The descriptive statistics of the sample demographics indicate that the sample is overly educated and disproportionately White and female. This limits the ability to generalize the findings of this study to the target population and population of interest. Additionally, the violation of the linearity and monotonicity assumptions led to a change in study design and analysis procedures.

    The limitations will serve as the foundation to introduce recommendations for future research which is addressed in Chapter 5. Additionally, Chapter 5 highlights similarities and differences between the findings of this study and similar research alongside implications for future research, theory, and practical applications. Chapter 5 concludes with a holistic reflection of the problem space solidifying the place of this study within the context of the professional world of research and practice.

Chapter 5: Summary, Conclusions, and Recommendations

Introduction and Summary of Study

The vast majority of people will be in a romantic relationship at some point in their life. Romantic relationships have the potential to meet a host of individual and societal needs including emotional support, physical intimacy, and reproduction. Unfortunately, romantic relationships also have the potential for physical and emotional harm ranging from challenging to severely abusive. Literature related to romantic relationship functioning implicates conflict interactions as a primary predictor of either relationship success or failure (Slatcher & Schoebi, 2017). Conflict, a point of disagreement, is inevitable in any type of relationship and the ability to manage and resolve conflict is essential for the health and functioning of a romantic relationship.

Conflict strategies are the categories of behaviors and the methods that individuals use to manage and resolve conflict. Compromise is considered a positive conflict strategy because the use of this strategy during conflict is associated with relationship and personal benefits (Zacchilli et al., 2009). Compromise, as a conflict strategy, involves collaborative problem solving, assertive communication, and allowing all parties to share thoughts, feelings, and goals related to the conflict. Alternatively, domination and interactional reactivity are negative conflict strategies, and their use is associated with decreased relationship commitment and satisfaction (Zacchilli et al., 2009). Hallmarks of these strategies include yelling, being verbally harsh or abusive, trying to be right, or trying to force the other party into a particular course of action. According to Karremans et al. (2017) mindfulness may improve conflict interactions between partners through increasing emotion regulation, resisting retaliatory and reactive behaviors, and increasing mental flexibility related to prioritizing relationship wellness over self-interest. A small amount of literature exists to implicate mindfulness as a way of improving romantic relationship conflict; however, the literature remains unclear as the specific mechanisms or even the presence of a statistically significant relationship between mindfulness and conflict strategy use.

The purpose of this quantitative associative correlational study was to determine if and to what extent a correlation exists between the five mechanisms of mindfulness identified in the Five Facet Mindfulness Questionnaire and the six conflict strategy subdomains identified in the Romantic Partner Conflict Scale used by adults in a committed romantic relationship living in the mid-Atlantic region of the United States. This study was based on a call by Harvey et al. (2019) to examine the relationship between mindfulness and romantic conflict strategy using a mindfulness measure which includes the non-judging facet of mindfulness. Additionally, Harvey et al. (2015) cites the lack of a non-reactivity facet of mindfulness as a significant limitation of that study which examined the relationship between mindfulness and romantic partner conflict. On a theoretical level, Karremans et al. (2017) recommended future literature explore the specific facet(s) of mindfulness which serve as the mechanism(s) for the influence of mindfulness on romantic partner relationships. This study addresses those significant limitations and recommendations to produce a study with empirical, theoretical, and practical significance.

Chapter 5 begins with a summary of the study conclusions and reflections for the purpose of orienting the findings from this study in the context of existing literature. Next, there is a detailed discussion of the practical and theoretical implications followed by recommendations for practice and research. The final section of this chapter is a holistic reflection of the problem space.

Summary of Findings and Conclusion

Overall Organization

This section is a review of the study findings as they relate to existing empirical and theoretical literature. Additionally, a small section at the end includes a reflection of the dissertation process. Following the reflection, the next sections detail the recommendations, study strengths and weaknesses, and recommendations. The final section of this dissertation will conclude with a holistic reflection of the problem space followed only by references and appendices.

The theoretical foundation for the mindfulness aspect of this study was based on the model of mindfulness developed by Jon Kabat-Zinn. Kabat-Zinn's model of mindfulness integrates traditional Buddhist teachings with contemporary psychology to identify non-judgement and present moment awareness as primary hallmarks of mindfulness (Kabat-Zinn, 2003). This model serves as the foundation for the Five Facet Mindfulness Questionnaire (FFMQ), developed by Baer et al. in 2006, details five mechanisms or traits of mindfulness. These traits are practicable skills which allows for practical application such as the development of interventions to build skills which increase overall mindfulness. The separation of mindfulness into traits also enables more specific research and recommendations based on the specific mechanisms of mindfulness which are responsible for the desired changes in mental health symptoms, social functioning, and personal wellness.

The theoretical foundation for the romantic partner conflict strategies dimension of the study is social exchange theory published by Albert Chavannes in 1898. The primary tenets of the theory include successful relationships predicated on mutually beneficial exchanges and conflict as any point of disagreement between two or more parties. As early as 1898, Chavannes acknowledges the importance not only of goods and services in exchanges, but also of affection and enjoyment of the other party or parties. Social exchange theory serves as one of the primary theories underlying the development of the Romantic Partner Conflict Scale (RPCS) published in Zacchilli et al. (2009). This scale, along with similar research and studies using this scale, identifies compromise as a positive conflict strategy subdomain and interactional reactivity and domination as negative conflict strategy subdomains. Positive and negative are used based on their association with relationship benefits and consequences primarily measured in satisfaction and commitment.

The remaining three conflict strategy subdomains (avoidance, submission, and separation) yield mixed results regarding relationship benefits and consequences (see Zacchilli et al., 2009) and typically do not result in statistically significant results related to mindfulness (see Harvey et al., 2015; Harvey et al., 2019). The hypothesis from Zacchilli et al. (2009) is that these conflict strategies are more nuanced, and the positive or negative consequence is reliant on the context within which the conflict strategy is used. The RPCS measures the presence of six different conflict strategies across a range of functional and dysfunctional.

The purpose of this quantitative associative correlational study was to determine if and to what extent a correlation exists between the five mechanisms of mindfulness identified in the Five Facet Mindfulness Questionnaire and the six conflict strategy subdomains identified in the Romantic Partner Conflict Scale used by adults in a committed romantic relationship living in the mid-Atlantic region of the United States. Five research questions with hypotheses were developed to align with the purpose of the study. To align the purpose statement with the sample data, the inclusion criteria were age (over 18), state of residence (mid-Atlantic US), and membership in a committed romantic relationship. The collected data consisted of 103 completed surveys comprised of demographic information, the FFMQ-15, and the RPCS. The findings from the study revealed statistically significant correlations between acting with awareness/interactional reactivity ($\tau_b(103) = -.230, p = .002$), acting with awareness/domination ($\tau_b(103) = -.195, p = .007$), describing/compromise ($\tau_b(103) = .241, p < .001$), describing/interactional reactivity ($\tau_b(103) = -.209, p = .004$), describing/domination ($\tau_b(103) = -.264, p < .001$), non-judging/interactional reactivity ($\tau_b(103) = -.274, p < .001$), and non-judging/domination ($\tau_b(103) = -.350, p < .001$). The results of the research questions and position within existing literature is discussed in this section.

Research Question 1 Results. The first research question for the study was:

RQ1: If and to what extent does a statistically significant correlation exist between acting with awareness and the conflict strategy subdomains used between adults in a committed romantic relationship?

H_o1: There is not a statistically significant correlation between acting with awareness and conflict strategy use between adults in a committed romantic relationship for the following subdomains:

- Compromise

- Avoidance
- Interactional Reactivity
- Separation
- Domination
- Submission

H_a1: There is a statistically significant correlation between acting with awareness and conflict strategy use between adults in a committed romantic relationship for the following subdomains:

- Compromise
- Avoidance
- Interactional Reactivity
- Separation
- Domination
- Submission

The findings confirmed that acting with awareness is negatively correlated with interactional reactivity and domination at a statistically significant level. The results of the Kendall's Tau-b yielded the results as $\tau_b(103) = -.230$, $p = .002$ for interactional reactivity and $\tau_b(103) = -.195$, $p = .007$ for domination. According to Botsch (2011), these are both moderately strong correlations. The null hypothesis was rejected for the interactional reactivity and domination subdomains of romantic partner conflict strategy. The null hypothesis was not rejected for the compromise, avoidance, separation, and submission subdomains because there is not a statistically significant correlation between the acting with awareness trait of mindfulness and these four subdomains of romantic partner conflict strategy.

Acting with awareness is one out of five facets of mindfulness identified in the FFMQ-15 which is clearly a parallel of the definition and model of mindfulness developed by Jon Kabat-Zinn. Mindfulness has an element of being *on purpose* (Kabat-Zinn, 2011). Kabat-Zinn's model of mindfulness and Mindfulness Based Stress Reduction program highlight mindfulness as not only a state of being, but also a practice. In this way, acting with awareness can be understood as doing things intentionally rather than acting out of habit or emotion (Kabat-Zinn, 2003). The ability to make intentional decisions becomes critically important during conflict interactions where emotions can become escalated. Delatorre and Wagner (2019) cite a commitment to problem solving as a hallmark of a constructive conflict strategy, and Karremans et al. (2017) cites attentional awareness as a facilitator of emotion regulation and maintaining goal focus during conflict. The results of this study confirm that as acting with awareness increases, domination, and interactional reactivity (negative conflict strategies) decrease with a moderate effect. This aligns with the theoretical literature related to acting with awareness and conflict strategies.

The literature identified in Chapters 1, 2, and 3 cites two research studies which used the RPCS alongside different mindfulness measures to examine the mechanisms underlying the relationship between mindfulness and romantic partner conflict. Harvey et al. (2015) reported the Pearson's *r* value as $r = -.21, p < .05$ for acting with awareness and domination. This was the only conflict strategy with a statistically significant correlation to acting with awareness as reported by Harvey et al. (2015). Harvey et al.

(2019) featured the use of the Mindful Attentional Awareness Scale to examine actor-partner effects of mindfulness and conflict strategy use. This study reported that higher levels of female mindfulness were correlated with lower levels of male partner domination and reactivity. This study aligns with the findings of similar empirical studies in the identification of a statistically significant negative correlation between acting with awareness and domination and interactional reactivity.

Research Question 2 Results. The determination that the data related to the observing facet of mindfulness is unreliable precluded analysis and ability to answer research question 2.

RQ2: If and to what extent does a statistically significant correlation exist between observing and the conflict strategy subdomains used between adults in a committed romantic relationship?

H_o2: There is not a statistically significant correlation between observing and conflict strategy use between adults in a committed romantic relationship for the following subdomains:
- Compromise
- Avoidance
- Interactional Reactivity
- Separation
- Domination
- Submission

H_a2: There is a statistically significant correlation between observing and conflict strategy use between adults in a committed romantic relationship for the following subdomains:

- Compromise
- Avoidance
- Interactional Reactivity
- Separation
- Domination
- Submission

The Cronbach's alpha score is a measure of internal reliability and should be at least .7 to indicate an appropriate level of internal reliability for a measure. The Cronbach's alpha score for the observing facet of mindfulness was α=.61 (see Table 4.12) indicating a substandard level of internal reliability. This is lower than the reported score of .78 in Meng et al. (2020), but similar to the result of .64 reported in Gu et al. (2016). There is also some support for excluding the observing facet from analysis models when working with a primarily non-meditating sample as is the case for this study. Gu et al. (2016) reports that while the five-facet structure is optimal when working with a meditating sample, a four-facet model which excludes observing is a better fit for a non-meditating sample. The same study also reports that the observing facet of mindfulness does not correlate significantly with the non-judging and non-reactivity facets of mindfulness. A possible explanation is that a person might be high in observing and low in non-judging and non-reactivity due to anxious monitoring or hypervigilance. Essentially, observing alone does not capture the curiosity, acceptance, and open awareness inherent in present-moment mindful observing.

Research Question 3 Results. The third research question for the study was:

RQ3: If and to what extent does a statistically significant correlation exist between describing and the conflict strategy subdomains used between adults in a committed romantic relationship?

H_o3: There is not a statistically significant correlation between describing and conflict strategy use between adults in a committed romantic relationship for the following subdomains:

- Compromise
- Avoidance
- Interactional Reactivity
- Separation
- Domination
- Submission

H_a3: There is a statistically significant correlation between describing and conflict strategy use between adults in a committed romantic relationship for the following subdomains:

- Compromise
- Avoidance
- Interactional Reactivity
- Separation
- Domination

- Submission

The findings from Kendall's tau-b suggest mixed results. The significant results include compromise ($\tau_b(103) = .241, p < .001$), interactional reactivity ($\tau_b(103) = -.209, p = .004$), and domination ($\tau_b(103) = -.264, p < .001$). The insignificant results include avoidance ($\tau_b(103) = -.045, p = .536$), separation ($\tau_b(103) = -.038, p = .603$), and submission ($\tau_b(103) = -.026, p = .723$). The null hypothesis was rejected for the compromise, interactional reactivity, and domination subdomains. There is a statistically significant correlation between describing and these conflict strategy subdomains identified in the RPCS as used by adults in a committed romantic relationship. The null hypothesis was not rejected for the avoidance, separation, and submission subdomains because there is not a statistically significant correlation between describing and these subdomains. This answered research question three.

Describing, as measured by the FFMQ-15, is the facet of mindfulness related to a person's confidence in their ability to use words to describe their inner experiences (thoughts, feelings, beliefs, fears, physical sensations) even while in distress. This facet of mindfulness is most directly related to communication. Karremans et al. (2017) cites awareness and communication of stressors as a requirement for building mutual support in the relationship. Therefore, ability to identify and verbally communicate internal (feelings, fears, insecurities) and external (stressors, demands on time and energy) factors is a requirement for building understanding, empathy, compassion, and collaborative problem solving. Similarly, Thomson et al. (2018) notes that attempting to inhibit or conceal emotions during conflict is associated with low conflict resolution. The findings of this study align with the theoretical understanding of the association between using words mindfully and conflict strategies.

Empirically, this study aligns moderately well with related findings from existing research. Harvey et al. (2015) reports statistically significant correlations for describing/compromise ($r=.22$, $p<.05$) and describing/avoidance ($r=-.21$, $p<.05$). Based on the theoretical and empirical evidence available, it was hypothesized that describing would be significantly correlated positively with compromise and negatively with avoidance, domination, and interactional reactivity; however, the results between describing and avoidance were not significant ($p = .536$) in this study.

Research Question 4 Results. The fourth research question for this study was:

RQ4: If and to what extent does a statistically significant correlation exist between non-judging and the conflict strategy subdomains used between adults in a committed romantic relationship?

H_o4: There is not a statistically significant correlation between non-judging and conflict strategy use between adults in a committed romantic relationship for the following subdomains:

- Compromise
- Avoidance
- Interactional Reactivity
- Separation
- Domination
- Submission

H$_a$4: There is a statistically significant correlation between non-judging and conflict strategy use between adults in a committed romantic relationship for the following subdomains:

- Compromise
- Avoidance
- Interactional Reactivity
- Separation
- Domination
- Submission

As with the previous research questions, the findings from Kendall's tau-b suggest mixed results. The significant results include results include interactional reactivity ($\tau_b(103) = -.274, p < .001$) and domination ($\tau_b(103) = -.350, p < .001$). The insignificant results include compromise ($\tau_b(103) = .156, p = .028$), avoidance ($\tau_b(103) = -.089, p = .220$), separation ($\tau_b(103) = -.095, p = .188$), and submission ($\tau_b(103) = -.146, p = .043$). The null hypothesis was rejected for the interactional reactivity and domination subdomains. There is a statistically significant correlation between non-judging and these conflict strategy subdomains identified in the RPCS as used by adults in a committed romantic relationship. The null hypothesis was not rejected for the compromise, avoidance, separation, and submission subdomains due to the statistical insignificance of the correlations. This answered research question four.

Non-judging is a facet of mindfulness which is taken directly from Kabat-Zinn's definition of mindfulness. According to Kabat-Zinn (2011), non-judging refers to the practice of not identifying with judgements and opinions, rather than the common misperception that judgements no longer exist. In this way, mindful non-judging is the experience of evaluations and opinions without feeling compelled to believe them as true or to react to them. Karremans et al. (2017) cites this mechanism of mindfulness as particularly important for managing romantic partners' inevitable shortcomings and annoyances. Judgement, when mismanaged, can lead to criticism and frequent conflict. When displayed during conflict, criticism and contempt are among the most harmful behaviors (Kim et al., 2007). In this way, non-judging is theoretically implicated to increase compromise and decrease domination and interactional reactivity; however, this study parameters determined the significance of the non-judging/compromise relationship to be insignificant. The significance was $p = .028$ which would be considered significant given other study parameters. This result may be interpreted as inconclusive.

  Empirically, the results for this research question align moderately well with the findings from similar studies. Harvey et al. (2015) reports statistically significant and negative correlations for non-judging/reactivity ($r = -.21, p < .05$) and non-judging/domination ($r = -.41, p < .01$). These results indicate that as non-judging increases, interactional reactivity, and domination decrease. The strength of the correlation is weak for interactional reactivity and strong for domination. Harvey et al. (2019) cites a limitation of their study as the use of a mindfulness measure which did not include a non-judging element. Non-judging is a widely accepted mechanism of mindfulness in both theoretical and empirical literature. Empirically, this study aligns precisely by determining the correlations between non-judging/interactional reactivity and non-judging/domination to be significant. The alignment with other literature increases the validity and reliability of these study findings despite the cited limitations.

Research Question 5 Results. The fifth research question for this study was:

RQ5: If and to what extent does a statistically significant correlation exist between non-reactivity and the conflict strategy subdomains used between adults in a committed romantic relationship?

Ho5: There is not a statistically significant correlation between non-reactivity and conflict strategy use between adults in a committed romantic relationship for the following subdomains:
- Compromise
- Avoidance
- Interactional Reactivity
- Separation
- Domination
- Submission

H_a5: There is a statistically significant correlation between non-reactivity and conflict strategy use between adults in a committed romantic relationship for the following subdomains:
- Compromise
- Avoidance
- Interactional Reactivity
- Separation
- Domination
- Submission

Unlike the results of the previous research questions, there were no conflict strategy subdomains which yielded a statistically significant correlation with the non-reactivity facet of mindfulness. The results are as follows: compromise - $\tau_b(103) = .185$, $p = .009$, avoidance - $\tau_b(103) = .059$, $p = .414$, interactional reactivity - $\tau_b(103) = -.176$, $p = .015$, separation - $\tau_b(103) = -.020$, $p = .777$, domination - $\tau_b(103) = -.178$, $p = .014$, and submission - $\tau_b(103) = .064$, $p = .374$. The results failed to reject the null hypothesis for each of the six conflict strategy subdomains because there is not a statistically significant correlation between non-reactivity and any of the six subdomains identified in the RPCS as used by adults in a committed romantic relationship. This answered research question five.

Non-reactivity is the facet of mindfulness addressing the ability to experience a situation, sensation, thought, or feeling without being compelled to follow a behavioral impulse to alter the stimulus. Kabat-Zinn (2011) cites reactivity as a primary characteristic of mindlessness, or the opposite of mindfulness. The traits of non-reactivity and non-judging combine to form the more complex state of acceptance which Karremans et al. (2017) define as the ability to be aware of something without needing to change or criticize it. In addition to the interpersonal implications, non-reactivity is also primarily implicated as the mechanism underlying emotion regulation. There are many stimuli, or opportunities, for escalation and reaction during a typical conflict interaction. Research on romantic relationships by the Gottmans and their associates demonstrate that it is possible to predict relationship outcomes based exclusively on the level of regulation displayed during conflict interactions (see Gottman & Levenson, 1992; Kim et al., 2007). Based on this theoretical evidence, acting with awareness is implicated to be positively correlated with compromise, and negatively correlated with domination and interactional reactivity. While the results demonstrated weak correlations which align with that implication, the significance of those correlations was not deemed statistically significant based on the study parameters (significance level set to .008 due to Bonferroni correction).

Empirically, it is worth noting that neither of the two frequently cited studies (Harvey et al., 2015; Harvey et al., 2019) featured the use of a non-reactivity mindfulness element. While not directly related to conflict strategies, other empirical studies report non-reactivity associated with lower levels of ruminating (Gu et al., 2016) and improved measures of well-being (Meng et al., 2020). The results of this study do not align with the existing empirical research suggesting that acting with awareness is an important mechanism underlying personal and relational benefits; however, this study identified 3 weak correlations at levels of significance just below the required level given the study parameters. This is discussed again in the recommendations for future research section.

Reflection on the Dissertation Process

There's a lot to be said for the expression, 'where the rubber meets the road.' The dissertation is the road, and the years of learning and seemingly endless classes are the rubber. Psychology classes, statistics classes, research methods classes all have their place, but nothing surpasses learning from experience. While traveling this road, I've had to replace several tires, as it were. Irreplaceable lessons include extracting variables and identifying a problem space from existing literature; using that literature to guide and bound a research design and all the methodological choices; and reading literally hundreds of articles to organize and write over 30 pages of literature review. The lessons never stop. It is human nature to say, 'after this, it will be easier'; however, life, and this dissertation, have shown that to be untrue. There are always challenges. Life is not about avoiding challenges or achieving a state perpetually free of challenge. Life is about building the tools and the community to face challenges anew each day.

Implications

The purpose of this quantitative associative correlational study was to determine if and to what extent a correlation exists between the five mechanisms of mindfulness identified in the Five Facet Mindfulness Questionnaire and the six conflict strategy subdomains identified in the Romantic Partner Conflict Scale used by adults in a committed romantic relationship living in the mid-Atlantic region of the United States. The results of this study contribute to the body of academic knowledge related to mindfulness and romantic partner relationships. This section includes implications for theory, practice, and research. The final section details the strengths and weaknesses of the current study which serve as the foundation for the recommendations discussed in the next section.

Theoretical Implications

The theoretical frameworks highlighted in this study are Jon Kabat-Zinn's model of mindfulness and Albert Chavannes's social exchange theory. This research study extends the use of social exchange theory as a model for romantic relationship functioning. Existing research related to romantic relationships suggests that increasing positive interactions and decreasing negative interactions is an effective strategy for improving relationships (Gottman & Levenson, 1992). Social exchange theory aligns with this research by purporting that a successful relationship is predicated on mutually beneficial exchanges. Conflict is inevitable and an example of an interaction. A mutually beneficial conflict exchange would be one which primarily consists of positive conflict strategies alongside minimal use of negative conflict strategies. Social exchange theory was originally developed as a sociological tool and referred to "successful societies" rather than successful relationships (see Chavannes, 1898). This research contributes to the literature extending the application of social exchange theory to romantic relationships.

Kabat-Zinn's model of mindfulness was selected as the theoretical foundation for the mindfulness dimension of this research study given the emphasis on both traditional and contemporary conceptualizations of mindfulness. Kabat-Zinn originally developed this mindfulness model to serve as the basis for his Mindfulness-Based Stress Reduction program (Kabat-Zinn, 2011). Since then, mindfulness has primarily focused on personal stress management, relaxation, and individual well-being. Karremans et al. (2017) confirms the popular focus on the individual benefits of mindfulness and points out that traditional mindfulness includes a focus on social connections, community, and relationships. The results of this study extend the use of Kabat-Zinn's model of mindfulness to conceptualize and explore the social effects of mindfulness. The operationalization of this model is discussed in the future implications section.

Practical Implications

Romantic relationships have the potential to be a source of support, positive experiences, comfort, and safety; however, there is also the potential for negative and emotionally painful experiences even when the relationship is not overtly abusive. Most people will exist in a romantic relationship at some point in their life because it is a part of the cultural life script and because humans seek out connections (Hoplock & Stinson, 2021). The potential for intense benefit or harm combined with the sheer universality of romantic relationships indicates the need to understand the factors influencing romantic function and dysfunction. Only through understanding the primary mechanisms influencing these interactions is it possible to develop interventions to improve relationship functioning. The literature review in chapter 2 includes a review of mindfulness and romantic relationships separately and concludes with a section on the points of convergence. These points of convergence along with the results from the current study serve as the basis for recommendations for future research and practice discussed in the next section.

The findings indicate a nuanced relationship between mindfulness and romantic partner conflict which precludes the conclusion of simply 'yes' or 'no' to the question of whether mindfulness improves romantic partner conflict. The purpose of this study to yield appropriate findings to make a cogent argument for or against the development of intervention tools featuring mindfulness to improve romantic relationship functioning. The mindfulness traits most significantly correlated with increased positive conflict strategy subdomains and decreased negative conflict strategy subdomains are acting with awareness, describing, and non-judging. This addresses the problem statement that it was not known if and to what extent a correlation exists between the mechanisms of mindfulness identified in the FFMQ and the conflict strategy subdomains identified in the RPCS.... Practically, this implies that application of mindfulness principles to improve romantic relationship functioning should focus on the acting with awareness, describing, and non-judging facets of mindfulness.

Future Implications

One primary implication for future research is the continued development and refinement of a mindfulness psychometric tool. Kabat-Zinn's model of mindfulness highlights features of mindfulness such as present-moment awareness, intentionality, resisting automatic impulses, and remembering that mental stories can be untrue and ignored (Kabat-Zinn, 2011). While there is a validated and reliable instrument available to measure mindfulness based on Kabat-Zinn's model (the FFMQ), the results from the literature review combined with the study findings indicate that some elements of mindfulness (kindness, curiosity, compassion) are missing from the psychometric tool. Mindfulness is a complex and multi-faceted concept with a host of varying definitions, so developing a psychometric tool which effectively captures each individually and holistically is a herculean task. The discrepancy between conceptualization and operationalization indicates the need for new research tools to accurately and reliably detect relationships between mindfulness and other constructs.

Other related studies have also cited an insufficient mindfulness measure as a limitation which reduces the validity and reliability of the conclusions. Harvey et al. (2015) cited the need for a non-reactivity facet, and Harvey et al. (2019) identified non-judging as a necessary component. This study featured a mindfulness measure with five facets in an attempt to capture all of the necessary elements of mindfulness. The results from the non-reactivity and non-judging facets provided significant insights and solidified their place as necessary elements of mindfulness alongside acting with awareness and describing. The lack of reliability in the observing component suggests that the conversion from conceptualization to operationalization requires additional research and development.

In addition to refining the mindfulness measure, the findings related to this study implicate the need for future focus on other types of research methodologies and designs. Three of the conflict strategies (submission, separation, and avoidance) have exceedingly mixed results related to relationship with mindfulness and correlation to relationship benefits and consequences. Integrating qualitative, mixed methods, and experimental designs would not only improve the understanding of these three conflict strategies, but also increase the understanding and practicality of findings related to mindfulness and romantic relationship conflict.

Strengths and Weaknesses of the Study

Strengths of the study include selection of the psychometric tools used to measure mindfulness and romantic partner conflict, anonymous survey design, recruitment strategy resulting in representation across age range and mindfulness level, and study alignment across theoretical and methodological choices. The psychometric tools (FFMQ-15 and RPCS) represent a strength in this study because they have documented validity and reliability and they align with similar studies in the field. Despite the observing facet of mindfulness being unusable due to low Cronbach's alpha score, this study highlights needed revisions to the questionnaire which is beneficial to the academic community. Anonymous survey design is a strength because it minimizes the risk for participants which could increase willingness to participate or to provide accurate responses. Self-report data is notorious for being biased by a participant's motivation to provide a 'desirable' answer, so having anonymous surveys may reduce that risk. The recruitment strategy involved shareable flyer-like posts on the researcher's personal page and approved Facebook groups. While the age and mindfulness dispersion was not equal across ranges, each age range was represented by at least one participant.

The final strength of this study is alignment across theoretical and methodological choices. The researcher began with a broad review of literature and identified patterns in theoretical frameworks, psychometric tools, research questions, and statistical analysis procedures. This led to the identification of the problem space and the development of the problem statement: It was not known if and to what extent a correlation exists between the five mechanisms of mindfulness identified in the Five Facet Mindfulness Questionnaire and the six conflict strategy subdomains identified in the Romantic Partner Conflict Scale used by adults in a committed romantic relationship. The FFMQ and the RPCS are primarily based on the theoretical frameworks of Jon Kabat-Zinn and Albert Chavannes. Karremans et al. (2017) specifically recommends future research examine the mechanisms of mindfulness as they relate to relationship outcomes. Quantitative methodology is predicated on the development and testing of hypotheses. The hypotheses for this study directly align with the research questions and purpose statement. The results of the data analysis procedures both answer the research questions and contribute significantly to the academic and practical body of knowledge related to the fields of mindfulness and romantic partner relationships.

There are also several weaknesses of this study. The first weakness of this study is the use of anonymous and self-report data which prohibits any verification of the accuracy of the reported levels of mindfulness and conflict strategy use. The survey also consisted exclusively of Likert-scale data which does not allow participants to explain their responses or allow the researcher to ask follow-up and clarifying questions. Participants also indicate their conflict strategy use retrospectively which has the potential for distorted reports. The survey had 7 demographic items and 54 survey items, so the length of the survey may also lower the quality and accuracy of responses.

Another weakness of this study was that the sample was not analyzed based on the influence of demographics. Addressing the influence of demographics is possible using hierarchical regression (see Harvey et al., 2015) or by comparing the results of analysis for two samples (e.g., meditating versus nonmeditating; see Baer et al., 2008). Limitations and weaknesses are unavoidable; however, it is crucial to consider them when interpreting the results of the study and when future researchers are planning additional studies. In hindsight, a between subjects design separating the sample into high mindfulness versus low mindfulness might have yielded results with more practical significance.

Recommendations

This research study examined the relationship between the mechanisms of mindfulness identified in the FFMQ and the conflict strategies identified in the RPCS. Based on that examination, several recommendations for future research and practice emerged. This final section of the dissertation outlines the recommendations for future research and practice followed by a holistic reflection on the problem space.

Recommendations for Future Research

The purpose of this research study was to examine the mechanisms of mindfulness as they related to conflict strategy subdomains to develop a cogent argument and recommendations for future research and practice. The data structure precluded the planned analysis and altered the available interpretations. Consequently, several research recommendations emerged as a result of theoretical and methodological limitations, delimitations, and weaknesses.

First, it is recommended that future studies use qualitative, experimental, or mixed methods research designs. The existing empirical literature on mindfulness and romantic partner relationships is almost exclusively reliant on self-report and Likert-scale data. It is probable that observations, interviews, focus groups, and field studies would provide a wealth of important knowledge with academic and practical significance.

Second, it is recommended for future research to explore the importance of including curiosity, kindness, and compassion in an operational mindfulness model. Kabat-Zinn (2011) discusses these elements as integral to the understanding and practice of mindfulness. It is important for future research to explore these as additional dimensions of mindfulness which may significantly alter the understanding of the way in which mindfulness interacts with other constructs. Similarly, future research is encouraged to continue to explore the context and relationships related to the non-reactivity facet of mindfulness as it did not yield statistically significant results during this study.

Third, it is recommended that future research focus on exploring and building an understanding of the nuances and relevant contexts underlying the mixed results related to the avoidance, submission, and separation conflict strategy subdomains. All three of these subdomains are correlated with both relationship benefits and consequences (see Zacchilli et al., 2009). This indicates that other factors influence the way in which these strategies affect individuals and relationships. These underlying factors could present key information in understanding and improving conflict interactions.

Fourth, it is recommended that research include both self-report and observational data. Self-report data is impossible to verify and therefore one must always use caution when interpreting the results. Research should include observation of partner interactions to verify use of mindful tools and conflict strategies (for an example of similar research, see Kim et al., 2007).

Fifth, it is recommended to include greater proportions of age, race, and gender diversity. Generalizability is specifically related to the ability of the research to describe the experiences of the target population; therefore, if the sample is not representative of the population, then it is likely that many people will not share the experiences of the sample. It is common for research to report demographic disparities and lack of diversity as a primary limitation. So future research should also include strategies to facilitate better inclusivity and diversity.

Sixth, it is recommended to account for the influence of demographics on the relationship between these variables. Harvey et al. (2015) demonstrates the use of hierarchical regression as one way to account for the influence of demographics. Chapter 2 identifies several demographic variables including gender, age, race, culture, and sexual identity which influence personal and romantic relationship functioning. Additionally, attitudes and beliefs about conflict influence conflict strategy use. These personal and demographic variables must be acknowledged and accounted for before accurate analysis can occur of the relationship between mindfulness and romantic partner conflict strategies.

Recommendations for Future Practice

As discussed in the previous section, the practical applications of this research are primarily concerned with the potential efficacy of a romantic relationship program featuring mindfulness-based interventions. Based on the results of this study alongside those of existing studies (see Harvey et al., 2015; Harvey et al., 2019), it is recommended that providers facilitating romantic relationship improvement should include the use of mindfulness skills which promote acting with awareness, describing, and non-judging. These mindfulness facets are supported by multiple studies, including this one, to be moderately and strongly correlated with increases in positive conflict strategies and/or decreases in negative conflict strategies.

Similarly, it is recommended that helping and teaching professionals should be familiar with mindfulness-based interventions. While mindfulness has grown in popularity over the past few decades (see Baer, 2019), there is still misconceptions about mindfulness and mindfulness practices which prevent many providers from using and teaching the skills. The literature review in Chapter 2 identifies some barriers to mainstream inclusion as a misperception of mindfulness as a religious practice and confusion in the academic community as to the specific definition or conceptualization of mindfulness. School teachers, healthcare professionals, and mental health professionals could all benefit from implementing the suggestions of this study through improved personal and professional interactions. Tekel and Erus (2020) supports the benefit of mindfulness-based practices for improving social interactions between teachers and students. Additionally, teachers, healthcare and mental health workers all interact with romantic partners (parents, married couples, etc.) on a daily basis, so having a foundation from which to improve stressful interactions is a worthwhile endeavor.

Conversely, it is recommended that mindfulness teachers, providers, and practitioners acknowledge and explore the social elements of mindfulness. In contemporary research and mental health, mindfulness is often criticized for increasing self-centeredness and arrogance (Dawson, 2021). A deeper understanding of the traditional background (provided in Chapter 2 and referenced in earlier sections of Chapter 5) of mindfulness makes it clear that a hallmark of a mindfulness practice involves directing non-judgement and compassion towards self and others. Karremans et al. (2017) cites the mindfulness writings of Buddhist monk Thich Nhat Hanh wherein the "miracles of mindfulness" include not only reducing personal suffering, but also facilitating a more loving connection with others.

A greater emphasis on the social benefits in addition to personal benefits is supported by this study and the existing academic literature. In doing so, this study can benefit not only those in a romantic relationship, but potentially society as a whole. Just as social exchange theory was reduced in application from society to romantic partnership, so too does the influence of the partner extend from their relationship to society. Individuals, families, and society exist in a reciprocal relationship whereby each affects the other.

Holistic Reflection on the Problem Space

Before this study, there was a gap in existing literature created by the methodological choices of previous studies. Harvey et al. (2015) identified the need to include a non-reactivity scale, and Harvey et al. (2019) identifies that a non-judging scale is a critical component when measuring mindfulness. This study is both an identification and remedy to these limitations cited in existing literature. This study featured the use of a mindfulness measure with the non-judging and non-reactivity facets alongside three other facets of mindfulness also supported by current literature as essential to a complete understanding, conceptualization, and operationalization of mindfulness. The use of a mindfulness measure with five facets also addressed the call from Karremans et al. (2017) to explore which mechanisms of mindfulness underlie the documented relationship between generalized mindfulness and romantic partner functioning. The results of this study implicate acting with awareness, describing, and non-judging as the primary mechanisms of mindfulness which are associated with better conflict strategy use.

The problem space identified in the literature is exemplified in the following statement. It was not known if and to what extent a correlation exists between the five mechanisms of mindfulness identified in the Five Facet Mindfulness Questionnaire and the six conflict strategy subdomains identified in the Romantic Partner Conflict Scale used by adults in a committed romantic relationship. This study found that very weak, weak, moderate, and strong correlations exist between identified mechanisms of mindfulness and conflict strategy subdomains. This study, when considered within the context of related theoretical and empirical literature, produced several notable implications and recommendations for future research and practice. First, there is adequate evidence to support research and development of mindfulness-based interventions focusing on the describing, acting with awareness, and non-judging facets of mindfulness. This is based on the evidence that these mechanisms are consistently correlated with an increase in compromise (a positive conflict strategy) and/or decreased domination and non-reactivity (negative conflict strategies). Second, additional research is recommended to explore the conceptualization, operationalization, and contextual position of the observing facet of mindfulness, and the separation, submission, and avoidance conflict strategy subdomains.

A primary recommendation is that research expand beyond self-report, quantitative analysis. Qualitative and mixed methods studies are recommended to explore the afore-mentioned mindfulness facet and conflict strategies given the existence of conflict findings from quantitative research. Experimental studies are recommended to explore causality between mindfulness and romantic partner conflict strategies. While this study highlights the need for continued research, the conclusion that acting with awareness, describing, and non-judging are consistently correlated with beneficial conflict strategy use is profound. This knowledge not only addresses a gap in the existing literature, but also identifies several other needs for future research and practice in the service of improving personal, relational - and by extension societal - outcomes.

www.ingramcontent.com/pod-product-compliance
Lightning Source LLC
LaVergne TN
LVHW011936070526
838202LV00054B/4669